The Blessing Of America, The Curse Of The Left, And The Scourge Of The Democrat Party:

Hard Hitting Truth Commentaries

By. Unpopular Politics

TABLE OF CONTENTS

INTRODUCTION

Why does the Democrat Party and the left in general speak so ill of the country? It's as though they are always trying to outdo each other in some kind of top this ridiculous statement, or let's see who can show more disdain for the country competition. America is not perfect. There are no perfect people so there is no perfect country, but is there another country that has worked as hard to move past the terrible aspects of its history than the United States?

Examine America's record, especially in the last one hundred and sixty years. Anyone would be hard-pressed to find another country in the entire history of civilization that has worked harder to become a fairer, better nation for all of its citizens. Much more than that, America has been successful beyond its wildest dreams, and today anyone can take advantage of the opportunities that exist here, and be successful.

None of that matters to the left and the Democrat Party. They insist that America is a racist cesspool where white supremacists want to reign supreme. It is a dung pit where women are subjugated, children are growing up without promise of a bright future. Old people are in danger of mass euthanasia and America is the most morally bankrupt nation that ever existed.

The left and the Democrat Party insists that all of that is true, and the only way to fix the dystopian hell hole that they imagine America to be is to turn absolute power over to them.

This book is a collection of random, varied thoughts, and reflections on these issues. The book is the author's attempt to point out how dangerous the left and the Democrat Party have become. It is not just to complain, but for people to see who they are, by giving cogent examples of how they have embraced evil, and use hysteria as an intrinsic feature of their destructive march.

In pointing out how dangerous the left and the Democrat Party are, maybe the book will open some eyes, and a few people will get in the battle to preserve the rich legacy that America's founding fathers have left us.

AMERICA THE BEAUTIFUL

The American Spirit

"Go west young man". Someone spoke these simple words over one hundred and fifty years ago. To go west meant the promise of an exponentially better chance of prosperity for the pioneers in a country that had not even scratched the surface of its unlimited potential.

There were no guarantees. There was only opportunity. Many accepted the challenge. The hardships encountered by the people making this trek are unimaginable by today's standards. Despite those difficulties, year after year, many uprooted their households to make the trip. Each family was responsible for themselves. During the journey, neighbors looked out for neighbors. There was no government or any type of public handout for the people who made the decision to embark on the journey. This never discouraged them though. In fact, it was never even a consideration. One common denominator among them was they were all imbued with a spirit of optimism. They had strong faith, and a can do attitude that suggested they could overcome and accomplish anything.

To give an idea of how difficult the journey was, here is a quote from one man during that era "To enjoy such a trip

… a man must be able to endure heat like a Salamander, mud and water like a muskrat, dust like a toad, and labor like a jackass. He must learn to eat with his unwashed fingers, drink out of the same vessel as his mules, sleep on the ground when it rains, and share his blanket with vermin, and have patience with musketoes … he must cease to think, except of where he may find grass and water and a good camping place. It is hardship without glory."

On top of all of this, they had to battle sickness and disease during a time when the study of medicine was still very primitive. These pioneers made many trips without people who even possessed the medical expertise of that time. They had to combat diseases like smallpox, cholera and tuberculosis, to name just a few. Many died and had to be buried along the way.

Among the problems they encountered were limited food supply, extreme weather conditions, river crossings, and numerous other challenges. These included conflicts with Native Americans. Despite all this, they persevered and blazed a trail that others would follow. Upon reaching their destination, the work did not stop for them. They then had to face the task of establishing and making lives for themselves in the newly acquired territory. Everyone literally had to start from nothing. All of them faced everything with a clear understanding that to be successful required making sacrifices and doing arduous work that they were willing to accomplish.

In today's America, it is common to hear that young people are jaded. They are discouraged and believe that the American dream is dead. Some say their future is bleak with less promise than those who came before them. How is this even possible? With so many amenities readymade and available to them, they complain about how tough their life is. Others have catered to them their entire lives. They have never known what it is to face an iota of the struggles that their counterparts from the aforementioned period of American history had to face.

They live in a world of gadgets that make so many things possible At no other time in the history has the globe been more linked. Cell phones make it possible for two people to talk at a minimal cost from opposite corners of the Globe. Information is available at people's fingertips. Education is open to anyone willing to learn. Trips across the country and around the world that would have literally taken months can now be done in just a few short hours at unbelievably low cost. However, people complain about their lack of opportunities.

It may be axiomatic to say that they do not understand how well they have it. Compared to the pioneers, they do not even have to battle so many diseases. This is not simply because medicine is vastly improved, but modern medicine has managed to eradicate some diseases that used to afflict us in the past.

There is free education. There are libraries and job training programs besides much public assistance worth tens of billions of dollars every year. People today have so many ways to amuse themselves. They have movies, plays, games, sporting events, museums, concerts, restaurants, and the list continues. It is tough to imagine how, in the midst of all this prosperity, so many can believe that the American dream is dead.

Perhaps what is missing in the discouraged generation is the can-do attitude of old, the eternal optimism, the faith in God and the rugged individualism that was the foundation of an earlier time. People had to provide for themselves and they knew that if they did not do it, no one would rescue them. This spurred them to action, and they accomplished remarkable things.

Today we must drive it into the minds of young people that opportunities still abound and that "the sky is still the limit" if they are only willing to open their eyes to see what is possible. They have to be willing to take risks in order to accomplish the impossible. They must believe in themselves and grab on to the many opportunities that are available to get themselves out of debt, find meaningful work, discover purpose, and lead the type of lives that they desire.

We have made it through many strenuous periods in this country's history, from the country's founding, through slavery to the civil war, reconstruction, Jim Crow, World War One, the great depression, World War Two, Vietnam, the civil rights movement, etc., all the way up to today's challenges.

In all of these, the one constant has been that we overcame them all. We can do the same against the challenges that we face today. In fact, we are in a better position to do so than at any other time in our history.

Religious Liberty

Congress shall make no law respecting an establishment of religion, or prohibiting the free exercise thereof. This statement is obvious, concise, and straight to the point. There is absolutely nothing in that statement that requires interpretation. There is not a single thing in the constitution that talks about the "separation of church and state." It is completely made up.

We can attribute the statement about church and state to a letter from Thomas Jefferson in response to members of the Danbury Baptist Association. These members of the association were worried about government encroachment on their religious liberties. He responded "Believing with you that religion is a matter which lies solely between man and his God, that he owes account to none other for his faith or his worship, that the legislative powers of government reach actions only, and not opinions, I contemplate with sovereign reverence that act of the whole American people which declared that their legislature should 'make no law respecting an establishment of religion, or prohibiting the free exercise thereof,' thus building a wall of separation between church and State".

It is interesting to note that two days after writing this letter Jefferson attended a church service in the House of Representatives.

Freedom of religion does not mean that there is no circumstance under which the practice of religion can be subject to certain laws. As a country though, we must be very careful how we choose to apply any rule of law against the free practice of religion. The government does not graciously grant this right to its citizens as an act of its benevolence. It is a God given right! And no one has the authority to impinge on it!

Just as no man has the right to enslave another, no one has the right to encroach on the religious freedom of another. It is significant that in countries where people are free to pursue their conscience as it pertains to religion, there tends to be respect for other freedoms as well. Religious freedom is strongly related to political liberty, economic freedom, and prosperity. "Wherever religious freedom is high, there tends to be fewer incidents of armed conflict, better health outcomes, higher levels of earned income, and greater educational opportunities for women."

Religious freedom is the harbinger of the many freedoms that people simultaneously enjoy. If you do not believe this, look at the countries where religion is forbidden or there is a theocratic state. The likelihood of countries like America suddenly descending into tyranny is highly improbable, but if it was to happen, it would most likely happen incrementally by attacking basic rights like religious liberty. For this reason, citizens must be vigilant and fight back against any, and all attacks on their faith if they want to continue enjoying this God given right.

The freedoms that we enjoy in the western world and other democracies directly result from this pioneering experiment in governance by the American people. We must ensure that these rights are there for, and continue to be enjoyed by our posterity.

The history of the world is littered with despots. Tyranny fills our not too distant past. We must be ever mindful of this. We must do everything in our power to guard these liberties that we take for granted. When Justice Hugo Black used the statement by Jefferson about church and state in his ruling against the school district in NJ almost 70 years ago, he started a dangerous precedent. Since then there has been a slow steady stream of subtle attacks on religious freedoms that have recently taken on new fervor. It has gotten to where one cannot even say a public prayer before a football game in many school districts. Some towns have banned traditional Christmas displays.

The United States government tried to force a major employer to provide the morning-after pills to women, even though it was against the beliefs of the employer. Some religious foster home charities have been forced to close their doors because they too refused to compromise their convictions about children growing up in traditional families. A city in California tried to ban home Bible studies. The state of Colorado has taken action against, and continues to harass a baker who does not cater to gay weddings, and the list continues.

What makes this particularly alarming is that the state has initiated these attacks under the guise of concern for some "broader" cause. Americans must be vigilant and guard against this slow invasive creep. Even if one hates religion and disagrees with many of the positions held by these religious institutions, no one can afford to let these attacks continue unchallenged. We are all stakeholders because, as religious freedom is affected, so are many of our other freedoms.

The Blessing Of America

We should never ever forget our history and all the terrible things that have occurred in the United States. Slavery contradicted the founding documents of the people who framed them.

For almost two hundred years, we failed to live up to the idea that all men are indeed created equal. The beauty of the founding documents though, is that they were created in such a way that it allowed us to apply remedies to that which did not live up to the founding ideals. As a result, we could successfully battle slavery, Jim Crow, beat the Klu Klux Klan, lynchings, peonage, integrate the military, integrate sports leagues, Brown vs Board of Education, etc., etc., etc.

With the passage of time, the United States has fought injustice, racism, inequality and other ills that have plagued society since the beginning of time. Keep in mind that before the United States, the way of the world was exactly what we fought to defeat. People lived their lives according to the whims of kings, monarchs, and tyrants. The rights that we enjoy in the world today and in the West is a gift given to the world by God through the United States and a handful of other nations.

While slavery was a scourge that plagued the world since time immemorial, it was the British, then the French, then the United States that gave freedom to slaves in a way that was never ever done before in human history.

Nations like Saudi Arabia abolished slavery in the 1960s. In Mauritania, they abolished slavery in 1981. In 2021 slavery is a scourge that still plagues the world. Many women and children are enslaved in the sex trafficking industry. As recently as 2017 in Libya, actual slave markets were thriving. In Sudan, there are enslaved people who can only dream of the freedom that we enjoy in America.

Today in America, we have grown so used to the way of life we have that we think it exists everywhere. We think this is the way it has always been. People need to be reminded that it is not, and it has not always existed in the way we have it in America today.

This is a very new experiment in history, no older than 250 years old in terms of the type of democracy that we enjoy today. It is the same in terms of the way that America and others in the world view slavery.

Despite all that America has achieved, despite all that we have done to correct the ills of the past, people continue to hold America's sins against the country. They cannot appreciate what we have now. The thing to keep in mind is this. As much as America has not always lived up to its ideals, there have always been people all along the way who hold the country accountable. These people fought to make the America into what we know it to be today.

During slavery there was the abolitionist movement and other examples of people rising to combat racism and other ills that prevented the country from achieving its full potential.

It is because of the promise of America that we passed the many civil rights bills that we have over the years. These bills got us to where we are today. The America of today is a world in which opportunity awaits everyone. Does racism exist? Sure! But there is no group of people in 2021 America who has to overcome what people in the 1960s, 70s, 80s, or 90s and earlier had to endure. The racism that exists is not enough to stop any group from achieving success by simply making use of the opportunities that are there.

That terrible things happen in life, including racism, is the consequence of living in an imperfect world where bad things are bound to occur. If no racism is the goal, then people will be disappointed for the rest of their lives. Racism, like greed, like hatred, like jealousy, sociopathy, and all the other reasons people do wrong things will be with us until the end of time.

We can choose to appreciate all the blessings that we have, and continue working to improve the society that we live in, or we can continue to live in grievance, upset that horrible things happen. This fantasy world where no racism exists is just that, a fantasy.

Independence Day And The Freedom It Represents

People often point to the indiscretions of the United States as examples of America's malevolence. What they fail to realize is that in a world where tyranny was the norm, and people all over the world were subjected to the oppressive whims of monarchs; the founders introduced a new system of governance to the world.

It was based on the principle that all men are created equal and endowed by their creator with certain inalienable rights. The rights we enjoy as human beings are not because of the benevolence of any government or ruler. Instead, we are endowed by our creator with these inalienable rights. As a result, no one can arbitrarily revoke these rights without due process, and only under mitigating circumstances.

This idea was a revolutionary concept, and the constitution that was based on it placed many limitations on the government. It stressed what the government is not allowed to do to its citizens. Freedom of the individual and the pursuit of happiness was a fundamental belief that guided this revolutionary system.

Though imperfect, this new form of government allowed the country to confront and rectify many of the troublesome problems that it faced. It allowed people to openly oppose injustice, to resist oppression, and defy attempts to subjugate its people. It is because of this unprecedented idea of government by the people and for the people that caused the country to agonize over issues like slavery (how many countries have fought a civil war over slavery)? Women's suffrage and other ignoble policies that were inconsistent with founding values.

The country has fought many battles and has overcome seemingly insurmountable odds to become the greatest human force for goodness in the world that has ever been known. By no means is this a flawless country, but perfection is an impossible standard. America however constantly works on making itself better. Some have taken to highlighting the imperfections of America to ironically call for more government control and involvement in the lives of citizens. They forget the history of tyranny by governments until this magnificent experiment in governance by the United States.

Today, many people are now willing to cede control of certain areas of their lives to the government for so-called security. They forget the beneficiary is always at the mercy of the benefactor. When this happens, a direct result is freedom comes under assault (observe current attacks on the first amendment). When faced with these threats even more vigilance is needed in order to ensure that we maintain freedom for posterity.

If we ever lose our freedoms, it will not happen overnight, but through a slow creep that then overtakes us before anyone can react. It was James Madison who said "Since the general civilization of mankind, I believe there are more instances of the abridgment of the freedom of the people by gradual and silent encroachments of those in power than by violent and sudden usurpation".

Remember also this quote by Ronald Reagan "Freedom is never more than one generation away from extinction. We didn't pass it to our children in the bloodstream. We must fight for it, protect it, and hand it to them to do the same, or one day we will spend our sunset years telling our children and our children's children what it was once like in the United States where men were free."

We must never forget the sacrifices of those who fought the intellectual, philosophical, spiritual, and physical battles in the name of freedom and most importantly, the values they lived that helped to shape and produce what has been, and continues to be the greatest force for progress in the world: the United States of America.

Always remember how much we had to overcome to get to where we are today.

Happy Independence Day.

The High Cost Of Freedom

The saying that freedom is not free is not just a pleasant sounding cliche. It is a harsh reality that bears witness in blood-stained fields across the globe, and in fatherless homes across the nation. Many other relatives and friends who will never again see their loved ones know all too well that freedom is not free. The bodies laid to rest in the hills of Arlington Cemetery are a poignant reminder of the cost that we pay to preserve freedom.

In this country's history, there have always been people willing to pay that ultimate price in defense of the freedom that we enjoy. This is something that so many others take for granted. Those who are the guardians of this liberty, that we have been blessed by almighty God to experience, have done such a marvelous job that many Americans think this freedom happens in a vacuum. They live their lives completely oblivious to the sacrifices and the severe toll that is required of those who have sworn to defend this freedom.

Some Americans even believe that the defenders of this freedom are the very cause of all the turmoil and the unrest in the world. They naively think that if America was to disarm, then the rest of the world would follow. This would be enough to eliminate war from the face of the earth. They are willingly ignorant of human nature. They turn a blind eye to history, and they disregard the norm of oppression that people suffered at the hands of monarchs and despots for most of human existence.

Many of these Americans who hold their country in such contempt fail to realize that this concept of freedom that they enjoy today is relatively new. It was America who ushered it into the world. There is however a group of Americans who understand, in the truest sense of the words, that freedom indeed is not free.

They stand ready to defend the rights of the naïve, the ignorant and the ungrateful. They willingly give their lives in defense of those who call them baby killers, war mongers, barbarians, and war criminals. Those who give their lives in defense of freedom understand what is at stake. Because of this they are not easily deterred by those who complain about America's powerful military.

They understand that in a world of imperfect people, no country is without flaws. They know that by standing in defense of liberty; they are also giving the nation the opportunity to be better. These valiant Americans have been constants in the nation's history. Whether it was facing off against the mighty British Army or battling their fellow countrymen for the cause of freedom, they were always there.

President Ronald Reagan, in a speech honoring the fallen, once paid tribute to one of these noble Americans. The young man's name was Martin A. Treptow. He gave his life at the young age of 26 in defense of freedom during the First World War. His attitude exemplified why, in such a short period, this country has accomplished so much more than any other nation before it.

Treptow's diary was found near him when he was discovered, and in it was a short piece he called "my pledge." It said: "America must win this war." Therefore I will work, I will save, I will sacrifice, I will endure, I will fight cheerfully and do my utmost, as if the issue of the whole struggle depended on me alone."

Mr. Treptow is just an example of why so many Americans can freely live their lives in blissful ignorance and ingratitude. It is the reason the flag burners, the anthem protesters, and America hating citizens can continue to express what is on their hearts without the fear of political repercussions.

As we look around the world, the evidence is everywhere that freedom is indeed not free. As Americans, we have the choice to complain about all that is wrong in the country. Or we can be thankful that we live in the freest, most prosperous country that has ever existed on the face of the earth. This does not mean that we have to ignore the areas where we need to improve as a nation.

The ability, and the willingness to identify actual problems where they exist, and then put systems in place to address them, is part of the legacy of those who gave their lives in defense of this great nation.

Let us honor their sacrifices and be thankful for all the blessings that we have as Americans.

Memorial Day, Why They Sacrificed Their Lives

"We hold these truths to be self-evident, that all men are created equal and endowed by their creator with certain unalienable rights, that among these are life, liberty and the pursuit of happiness. That to secure these rights, Governments are instituted among men deriving their just powers from the consent of the governed."

The idea hat gave birth to America was unheard of at that time. It was a brand new concept of governance. Until that time, people's lives were subject to the whims of monarchs, tyrants and the ruling class.

People questioned the legitimacy of the ruling class to their own peril. Then out of nowhere, a group of upstarts introduced this new concept that Governments are accountable to the people, and that people have the right to change their Government when the Government fails the people. The idea in itself was revolutionary, and if allowed to take root, would greatly upset the status quo and cause major problems for the ruling class.

The founding fathers declared independence based on the ideas found in the declaration of independence and broke their ties to the British Empire. The mighty British empire could not allow these ideas to become established and they sent their powerful military to ensure that they did not.

Standing in the way of the British though, was a small group of men who believed so strongly in their ideas that they were willing to die for them. Many of them did. This began the process that has led to the country that we have today. To get here, we have always had to call on the select few who would fight for, and even give their lives to preserve the ideals on which the country was founded.

The founding fathers and their posterity continued to build on the principles that were at the heart of their revolutionary ideas. Built into the system that they developed were the mechanisms that allowed them to continue improving on policies that were unjust. With these novel ideas and the way of thinking, America made tremendous forward strides politically, economically, socially, militarily and in other ways, at an unprecedented pace.

Quite frankly, the world had seen nothing like it before nor since. The concept that all men are created equal and that freedom is a gift, and a right from God, not the Government, allowed mankind to thrive as never before. Nations that adopted aspects of America's system experienced similar prosperity.

In stark contrast, places that outright reject these principles experience the extreme opposite. People live in poverty, corruption is widespread, people fear for their lives, curable diseases still wreak havoc on the health of citizens. They often have much lower mortality rates.

Today, as America remains the most prosperous and free nation that the world has ever known, many Americans wake up each day without a thought of what is required for them to continue enjoying the freedoms they have, and the prosperity they enjoy. The lives we lead in America are often not fully appreciated by those who complain about all that's wrong in America.

The standard of living that we are blessed to have simply did not exist before this magnificent American experiment. This is how good life is in America! It is so good that because it is not perfect, many think that they live in a fundamentally unjust society. In other words, they hold the country to a standard of perfection that is impossible to meet.

Americans who think this way have the right to do this. Those who take for granted the life that they live can do so because of those who stand as the guardians of our way of life. Those who stand ready to defend this nation are prepared to do it against all enemies, whether these enemies are foreign or domestic.

While people literally sleep, oblivious to the dangers in the world all around them, there are men and women who put their lives on the line every day to keep Americans safe. America's history is filled with men and women of this calibre. They were present in the battle of Lexington, and they were there again at the battle of Louisiana when a few rag tag citizens resisted and pushed back the mighty British Military one more time in their second attempt to teach these upstart Americans a lesson.

The grit and determination of these Americans committed to keeping their countrymen safe was demonstrated by the "lost battalion" in the Argonne Forest, and in trenches across Europe in world war one. They stormed the beaches of Normandy in World War two. Many of them never made it back alive. They gave their lives on the Korean Peninsula during the forgotten war. When the nation was divided, they gave their lives in the Jungles of Vietnam. The story is no different today as many families mourn the loss of loved ones killed in Iraq or Afghanistan.

Some say all that we need is for everyone to put down their arms and no one will ever have to die in needless wars and conflicts again. This naïveté ignores what we know about human nature. Human beings have a propensity toward violence and evil in general. Many have no problem giving in to this tendency. Whereas in a perfect world there would be no need for armies, the reality is that we do not live in a perfect world. In this reality, we will continue to depend on those who we memorialize on this day. As we honor the memory of those who die in service to our country, let us not forget our law enforcement officers. They also give their lives to keep our citizens safe.

The Realities And The Aftermath of War

People often forget that a soldier's mission is to fight and win the nation's wars. They forget that war is a brutal, savage endeavor. In the confusion, the chaos and the fog of war, men are called on to make split-second decisions about hurting other human beings, and the slightest bit of hesitation can get one killed or maimed. To survive requires a mindset that puts in gear the classic "kill or be killed outlook". It is a dark place. Only those who have gone there can truly understand.

During the Iraq war, there was an outcry when cameras captured Marines firing on an enemy combatant who appeared to be wounded, lying on the ground, and not a threat to anyone. What the cameras did not capture and people did not know was that after that battle, some combatants continued to attack while pretending to be dead or wounded-and while being truly wounded.

The people sitting in judgement in TV land saw cruelty. The men in the midst of the battle had to make a quick judgement call and respond to what appeared to be another wounded combatant preparing to fire on them. It is easy for people to lose sight of these harsh realities when sitting thousands of miles away in the comfort of their living rooms.

Many people spout cute sounding cliches, such as "war is not the answer" and "make love, not war." They philosophically declare "nobody wins a war," but in a world where evil exists, these cliches mean nothing. The aggressive use of force is sometimes necessary to deter evil, and give peace a chance to thrive.

Make no mistake about it. Soldiers do not delight in war, for "it is the soldier above all others who prays for peace, for it is the soldier who must suffer and bear the deepest wounds and scars of war" (General Douglas McArthur). On 6 June 1944, allied forces led by American Soldiers were called upon to bear the scars of war in a battle unlike before it. Young men said goodbye to family, friends, fiancés and other loved ones in their lives, to answer the call. They understood they might never see their loved ones again.

Many paid the ultimate price by answering that call. Others came back permanently scarred. They never attempted to shirk the heavy burden that they were called to bear, but responded to the sense of duty that they had. These men knew they had the full support of a grateful nation. They understood that their cause was just, and they gave their all confronting evil, and in defense of freedom.

No one back home was protesting the war. The concept of American might offended no one. There were no peaceniks demanding that we give diplomacy a chance. Americans understood we needed a decisive victory. The allies defeated Hitler's Army at a costly price and liberated the people who were held captive by his iron grip. The world soon learned the shocking depths of depravity to which people can sink when the plight of the Jews in the Holocaust became known.

America's fighting forces are the most compassionate. Their grit and determination have shown the world that freedom is worth the ultimate price. America, like individuals, is not without faults, but America is the greatest human entity for good in the world, while also vigorously and unapologetically pursuing its interests (as it should).

The sacrifices that America's servicemen and women have made the world over has helped to usher in an era of prosperity in the different regions of the world that they have liberated. Western Europe experienced unparalleled economic growth, peace, political and economic stability. Germany became the third biggest economy in the world and the mecca of engineering. Japan rose to become an industrial giant and economic power, becoming the second biggest economy in the world.

After the surrender of Japan, and the United States Military took control of South Korea. They sacrificed another fifty-five thousand soldiers in defense of South Korea five years later to beat back the forces of the invading North Korean Army. South Korea eventually became the fourth largest economy in the world and the premier ship builders on the planet.

Compare the countries where there continued to be an American presence and the countries where the Soviet Union remained. Look at North Korea today, East Germany during the split of the country, the countries that formed the Warsaw Pact and African Nations that aligned themselves with Russia/The Soviet Union. All of these countries experienced unprecedented misery, suffering, economic disaster, political chaos and corruption. There are no success stories!

It is interesting to note that the two American Military campaigns where no American Military presence was left or significant aid continued, both countries soon also became catastrophic failures. On both occasions liberal politicians sabotaged the Military effort in pursuit of their ideology, and the desire to embarrass their political opponents. Despite American soldiers being portrayed as barbarians, scenes of the war being beamed nightly to living rooms, and people calling for withdrawal from Vietnam, American soldiers were able to draw the Vietcong to the negotiating table. America forced them to concede, and got them to sign the Paris Peace Accord in 1973.

America left Vietnam but continued providing military aid to the South in order to keep the North at bay and ensure they upheld their part of the agreement. After the peace agreement was signed, a liberal Democratic congress swept into power in the United States and they cut off military aid to South Vietnam. With no more military aid to the South, the North resumed their attacks and South Vietnam fell. The slaughter of five million people in the killing fields of Laos and Cambodia followed the fall of Saigon. Some dispute this had anything to do with the fall of Saigon, but the left's undermining of the whole effort eventually led to the fall of the Vietnamese Government. It was a losing effort for a long time.

To liberal politicians, their ideology was more important than the sacrifices made by America's Service men and women, and more important than the slaughter of those millions of people. True to form liberals would give a repeat performance during the Iraq war. After voting to send more

Americans into harm's way based on information they had, they then did everything in their power to sabotage the war effort.

Who can forget the words of Harry Reid when he stood up on the Senate floor and said, "Mr. President, this war is lost." Once again, the prowess of American fighters prevailed, and they gained another victory for their country. Once again, liberal ideology trumped the sacrifices made by our Armed Forces. After so much blood and sacrifice, American troops pulled out of Iraq. Iraq quickly regressed into chaos and the scourge of ISIS was borne.

Recently, someone wondered aloud if the victories of World War two would be possible today. With the carnage, the savagery, the deaths of civilians and all the other catastrophic side effects of war being broadcast on TV every night, how would the American public and politicians react today? As America reflects on the sacrifices of those brave men who stormed the beaches of Normandy seventy-five plus years ago, remember that they were successful because they were given the tools that they needed to succeed, perhaps the most important tool being the political will to follow through on the commitment that its leaders had made.

Never forget, on Memorial Day and every day.

THE AMERICA HATING LEFT

The American Divide

There was a time in the United States of America when the people had a common love of the country. They agreed that even though we had problems, we live in a great place with the freedoms, privileges, and amenities that we enjoy. People understood that the country had serious issues that it needed to work out. They understood implicitly that in the history of the entire world, going all the way back to antiquity, there has never been a more successful experiment in governance than in the United States.

The beauty of America is that the principles on which the country was founded are very upright. In the areas where we did not live up to them, the people had systems in place to make them right. That is why in a world where slavery was the norm, the people were able to force change. They argued that the Judeo/Christian principles the founding fathers often referenced were not compatible with slavery and other injustices. They corrected it as a result.

Unlike in the past, when people were governed according to the whims of monarchs, and the so called "divine right of kings" superseded the rights of everyone else, America took a different approach. The voice of the people mattered more than the voice of any one individual.

Because this experiment has been so successful here, and spread successfully to other parts of the Western world, people mistakenly think that it has always been this way. Many do not appreciate how blessed we are, and they judge the country based strictly on its imperfections. They measure who we are against a standard of perfection. This means that no matter how far we've come, no matter how much adversity we've beaten, they only see the negative things that ail us.

It is because so many have been raised to judge the country based on its imperfections that there is no longer a common appreciation of the country that Americans once shared. There were always differences of opinion in terms of what we need to do to keep improving as a society. However, there was a bond that people had as fellow Americans.

Today there is a major political Party whose entire platform is based on vilifying the country, and their fellow citizens. At every opportunity they get, they tell us that one group of Americans harbors feelings of ill will towards other groups of Americans, for no other reason than differences in the color of their skin. They tell us that certain groups of young men have to legitimately fear for their lives because the country hates them. This political party tells everyone that there is a system in place designed to deny these young men their civil rights. Members of this party insist that the police wantonly take their lives of black men for no other reason than the color of their skin.

When they were not in power, they and their supporters told us every day that the President of the United States is a racist. He is a white supremacist. He is a Nazi. They told us that the then President of the United States hates women, and the reason he could get so much support is because the people he appeals to share his ideology of hatred. They have even labeled "people of color" who supported the President as white supremacists. It did not matter what time of the day it was, there was a constant barrage of negativity from people who believe that anyone who does not share their vision for the country is by nature a really terrible human being.

These people think that there is no reason to be proud Americans. Patriotism offends them. The idea of standing for the national anthem and saluting the flag is offensive to them, and saying the pledge of allegiance is now considered to be insultive to them.

Who would have ever thought that, but it is the current reality. Chanting "USA, USA" is a racist "dog whistle" to many. They shake their heads in disapproval whenever they see or hear what they consider being such acts of false patriotism.

In that environment, it was absolutely refreshing to have someone in the white house who was a cheerleader for the country. Baseless charges of bigotry did not cower Donald Trump into silence. His supporters understood that there are real problems in the country, but they also recognized that the country has built-in mechanisms to help us overcome the problems that we face as a nation. Most of all, they understood how blessed they are to be a part of this great and blessed nation.

Death To America

Death to America! Death to America! Death to America! Death to America!

That's the infamous chant that rings out from the squares in the Islamic Republic of Iran. Iran is the main state sponsor of terrorism around the globe. They oppress their people with a heavy hand and they are the main destabilizing force in the Middle East.

Death to America!

But just in case you are wondering, know this. In the last year, some shouts of the hateful anti-American slogan were not coming from the voices of the imams. Those chants were not coming from the people those imams usually lead in the shout all the way from Azadi Square.

No sir, in August 2020, some of those squawking chants of death to America were coming from the mouths of Black Lives Matter and their supporters in the enlightened city of Oakland in the state of California. Displaying hatred for their country and its institutions is how they hoped to inspire people.

No one was surprised though. These are the same people who once chanted in the streets "what do you want…dead cops…when do you want em…now!" Another time they waxed poetic and chanted "pigs in a blanket, fry em like bacon." The media never once condemned their despicable rhetoric, in fact; members of the media made excuses for them. That was not Black Lives Matter. They were not really threatening the police, cried the media. The media was out there like a bunch of bush lawyers making a case for the obstreperous fools.

With time, these ungrateful, spoiled, anti-American children only became more emboldened. At one time during one of their events, they boldly, without fear of negative consequences, told "journalists," "white reporters go to the back" to make space for reporters of color. The white journalists dutifully obeyed without an ounce of push back.

For anyone who wants to know what this destructive, poisonous movement called Black Lives Matter is all about, they have told us in the past. They want to disrupt the nuclear family, free abortions, the abolition of the police, an end to capitalism, plus other extreme goals. They seem to champion the cause of anything that rips away from the fabric of the black community.

This Black Lives Matter nonsense is a cancer that is only fomenting discord in the nation. The movement is based on lies and one of the most grand delusions ever perpetrated. Convincing Americans that black people, black men in particular, are under siege in America is one of the biggest scams of all time.

Black Lives Matter were the people wreaking havoc in Democrat cities across the country. As they walked along, they left a trail of blood, violence, mayhem, and death. Democrat politicians have refused to speak out against them, so they continue on their destructive path.

In 2020, during one of the most brazen, shameless displays ever, after encouraging violence, lawlessness and refusing to call out the mob for over six months; Democrat politicians flipped the script. They then started complaining, and trying to blame Trump supporters for the chaos Democrats encouraged in their own Democrat cities for months on end.

It was real Twilight Zone stuff. We still seem to live in some kind of alternate reality, where up is down, in is out, front is back, and wrong is right.

Craaaazy!

Being Unpatriotic Is The New Cool

When and how did it become cool to be unpatriotic? All across America, people seem to be competing against each other to see who could show the most contempt for their country. What is so terrible about the United States of America that makes so many of its own citizens feel the need to show so much disdain to the country that offers them so much?

The ingratitude that so many people who live and prosper here have towards the country is a phenomenon that is truly perplexing. The sheer disdain that so many people have towards the country is absolutely mind-boggling. All across the country in college campuses, students burn the American flag because they say it is a symbol of hate, racism, and bigotry. They have slogans like "America was never great," F**** your flag, some symbolically use the flag as a toilet rag. Others state that they have no reason to be proud of America.

How is it that people born in the freest country ever, where people have the opportunity to do so much for themselves to make their dreams become a reality, could have so much scorn for their own country? These people cite all that is wrong with the country, and they point to all that they perceive to be unjust as reasons to deride the nation that has been so blessed by God, and in which they have the privilege to live.

All across the country there are people embracing the status of the victim, and assuming the mantle of the aggrieved so that they can then say what an awful country America is. Being a victim is now a badge of honor for many. This stuff is absolutely amazing to watch.

Even some people who come here from other countries and live lives they never would have dreamed possible in their own homelands get in on the America bashing game. Despite the fact that America is always working to improve, and make the country a better place for all of its residents and citizens, all that you ever hear about from some citizens is how terrible a country this is.

For many, the only way to appreciate their country is for it to be perfect. Many of them have been fed a steady diet of anti-American sentiment from their earliest days, and on college campuses. It is to where America hatred is firmly entrenched in their hearts. Even as they breathe the air of the freest country in the world's history, and they reap the benefits of being Americans, they complain they are oppressed and deprived.

So many refuse to celebrate what they have. They whine incessantly about what they don't have. Instead of being thankful for all the mechanisms that are in place to address injustice, people complain that injustice exists. Instead of celebrating the many opportunities that there are for people to climb out of poverty, they complain that there is poverty.

This pattern can be seen in the way that many of them talk about America's past. When they talk about slavery, it is always in the context of how evil America was. However, they always cannot give America any credit for being one of the first nations to abolish the institution of slavery. They remain cynical and refuse to see the tremendous good that America has done in the world.

At the risk of sounding like a broken record, this must be said again. So many people do not know what the world was like before the American experiment. They think that the version of the world we have today always existed. What they fail to realize is that before America, the world was a totally different place.

America introduced to the world the concept of government, for and by the people. America instituted a form of government that stated our rights come from God and not governments. It is only as America became a nation, that the freedoms we know and enjoy today eventually became commonplace around the world.

It took time to get to the place where we are today, socially and politically. From the birth of the nation to today, America has always worked to improve itself. As the country has become more enlightened, it has embraced the principles of an enlightened society. She is still not perfect, but no country in the world is perfect, just as there are no perfect individuals.

Society will always reflect the people who make it up. The imperfections that exist in any society are not necessarily what defines the society. What and how they address those imperfections to become better is the mark of a really decent society.

Has there ever been a nation so blessed, where such a large number of its people are not grateful for, neither do they know or understand what they have and how blessed they are?

The Stunning Ungratefulness Of Americans

Has there ever been a people in the world's history more ungrateful than Americans, particularly those in the Democratic Party and the left? How, when, and where did it become so cool to denigrate one's own country?

It is absolutely amazing to watch so many citizens of this country take such pleasure in bashing the place that makes it possible for them to prosper and live lives of freedom, like no country ever has before. Despite the many opportunities that continue to be available to all who will put forth the effort, and take advantage of the opportunities, the Democratic Party continues every single day to spew hatred toward the land that has given it's citizens, and the world so much.

The mantra is basically that America stinks. One never hears any praise or thankfulness to God for the many blessings they enjoy as Americans. These people wake up every day and compete to outdo each other in expressing their contempt for the country. They pride themselves on not being proud to be Americans. This absolutely boggles the mind.

They harp on everything that is wrong with the country and ignore the good. They thrive on unhappiness and get a kick out of being anti-American. But wait, they are not content to bask in their anti-American sentiment and hatred for their country. They now want to normalize it. They get angry at people who call them out on their behavior. Where is this stuff coming from? It is just plain unbelievable and leaves many people in a state of astonishment.

In order to appeal to a large segment of their base, politicians in the Democratic Party now use anti Americanism as a legitimate tactic in their overall strategy to win people over to their side. What can one say about that, except, WOW! How sick is that? Just incredible! Imagine that saying the pledge of allegiance in schools is now considered being controversial in many school districts across America.

A while back, no less a person than Hillary Clinton heaped praise on an eleven-year-old girl for kneeling during the pledge of allegiance. In a display of sheer self-aggrandizement, puffed up arrogance, and unmitigated disdain for their country, rich millionaire athletes refused to respect what has always been a revered tradition, and a moment of solidarity, to pay homage to the country. They refused to stand for the playing of the National anthem. As these players stuck their collective middle finger in the faces of so many of their fans, while bringing their divisive, controversial politics to the workplace, politicians in the Democrat Party pandered to the ingrates. These politicians told them they can think of nothing more American than their show of disrespect when they dishonor the flag.

A few years ago, a former Army Captain playing in the NFL came out on the field during the National Anthem and paid his respects while his team mates stayed in the locker room. After receiving praise for refusing to swim downstream with the rest of the dead fish, the next day; this former Army ranger apologized to his teammates for "throwing his team mates under the bus." He said his teammates would have joined him if they knew he was going to go out there by himself. The fact that it was an issue at all speaks volumes.

This is all happening on the left, and in one political party. The Democratic Party! It is politics based on grievance. It is almost as though we have entered some kind of alternate universe, or a twilight zone type of existence. Another thing that is most amazing to see is that many immigrants have also chosen to adopt this anti-American attitude after leaving the land of their birth, and settling here to make a better life for themselves and their families. In a colossal twist of irony, many now seek to remake the country into that which they fled when they left their homeland, by espousing policies that drove their own countries into the dust.

When a couple of Democrat Party politicians were aspiring to be the next governor of New York a while back, they put on a show for the ages. For the entire debate, they threw out the most outlandish statements in what descended into a game of "top this insult." Governor Cuomo described agents of the Immigration and Customs Enforcement agency as thugs. One week earlier, he said, "We are not gonna make America great again. It was never that great. We have not reached greatness. We will not reach greatness until every American is fully engaged. We will reach greatness when discrimination and stereotypes against women, fifty-one percent of our population is gone."

Cuomo later apologized. He said that America is great, but he was inarticulate in the way he expressed his remarks. During the debate with his Democrat opponent Cynthia Nixon, she chided him. She took him to task for making the statement, then apologizing later because as far as she was concerned, America was never great. This is just a small sample of the crazy left and your modern Democrat Party ladies and gentlemen. Their view of America is imperfect, therefore America is an awful, oppressive, evil society.

No need for gratitude!

Anti-Americanism Reigns On The Left And The Democrat Party

Folks, one more time, just to drive it home. How do you reconcile that a significant number of people in one of the major parties in this country gets offended by displays of patriotism? What do you say about that? These people get offended by chants of USA, USA. They fret over saying the pledge of allegiance, and the United States flag is a symbol of oppression to them. They cheer for people who burn and dishonor the flag. They jeer at those who show reverence for that which the flag symbolizes.

This is your modern Democrat party ladies and gentlemen. The alarming thing though is that a lot of the madness that we witness in the Democrat party every day comes from leaders in the Party. It is crazy to think that in America today, the love of country is now controversial to so many people, including leaders in one of the major political parties

You have people like Congresswoman Ilan Omar who is a refugee. This country rescued her, but every time she opens her mouth to speak about America, she speaks with contempt for the land that rescued her. You'll be hard pressed to hear her say a positive thing about the nation that has offered her so much, and has been so kind to her. Ironically though, this is what makes her attractive to many of the people in the Democrat Party.

Apart from all of this, members of the Democrat Party constantly proclaim a message of gloom and doom, and speak as though nothing constructive ever happens in America. So it is confirmed! To be a true Democrat, one has to hate the country. To hear Democrat politicians and their minions speak, one would think that we are living in the middle ages under the tyrannic rule of some feudal lord.

My goodness, do these people appreciate anything about this place? If you listened to the Democrat debate from the last election, you would understand better. All 20 of the Democrat candidates told us over and repeatedly how terrible life in America is. Nothing is working right if you had asked any of those people. It was just a constant barrage of negativity coming out of the mouths of every single one of them.

It is unbelievable to watch people so privileged and blessed to live in a country like this do nothing but bash their country. Those Democrats on the debate stage told us that nothing encouraging is happening in the economy. They told us that people are dying all across the land because of evil insurance companies. Doctors are only interested in money. Corporations are evil money grubbers whose only interest is oppressing workers. They will have you believe no one is doing well in America. Tax cuts only benefit the rich. The rich are oppressing the poor, and the only reason that the poor are poor is because the rich are oppressing them.

According to Democrat politicians, no one experiences hardship in their life simply because they live in an imperfect world where things sometimes just go wrong. No sir that is never the case.

If anyone is holding out for a message of hope, or inspiration from the Democrat party, that person had better pull out a pair of high quality binoculars, and start looking for flying pigs.

The Democrats have made it clear that they do not wish to inspire anyone with a positive message of hope. Democrats tell us that oppression is everywhere and there is not a thing that anyone can do about it, unless people vote Democrats into power. We know firsthand what that entails.

The Value Of Your Story

There was a time when people had individual stories to tell. They told their story with gratitude for having been through it. While going through their experiences, they thought it would never end. However, many came up with inventive ways to make it through tough times. Many mothers have used the experience of struggling through hard times to teach their children thrift. These mothers have used their experience to teach their children thankfulness. They've taught them to sacrifice. They have taught them compassion towards others and several other life lessons. They tell stories of working two, sometimes three jobs. They talk about standing out in the cold early in the morning time and returning late in the evening to prepare dinner for the family, then getting ready to do it again the next day.

Many of these people would tell you that their experience was rough. They will tell you that while suffering through it they longed for change, but they used their situations to motivate themselves to do better. They did not whine, but educated themselves. They used the challenges they encountered to bring out their entrepreneurial spirit and inventiveness. They used challenges to claw themselves out of their difficult circumstances.

Dr. Benjamin Carson will tell you that his mother at one time could not read, but she knew she wanted a better life for her children. To help make this happen, she paid attention to the habits of the successful people for whom she worked and tried to copy them. She did not blame her dire situation on others. Instead, she learned valuable lessons that she applied to her own life. She emphasized the benefits of education to her children. The sacrifices that she made and the lessons that she instilled in her sons bore fruit. They grew up to be successful men, making significant contributions to the world.

Mr. Carson says that his mother never used her situation to embark on an excursion to Pityville. She instead she used it to drive her (all while raising her boys in the inner city). She accepted public assistance, but never relied on it as a means to stay where she was. It was not an automatic option, people usually resorted to it after all else had failed. As Dr.

Carson states, there was a stigma attached to accepting government handouts in those days and his mother worked hard to get off public assistance.

How many times have old timers intrigued us with their stories of their hardship? Many of them would recall their tales of privation with pride. They are mindful of how it helped to shape their character and prepared them to face life. They understand it is not a bed of roses, that sometimes it is unfair, and that at other times, life just happens.

For a lot of these people, a common thread that runs through their experience is a dogged determination to make it out of their circumstances. They do not blame others for their predicament. With a tenacity that stares obstacles dead in the face, they are optimistic that they will overcome them all.

This attitude is most demonstrable in the attitude of the pioneers from the early days of America's history. These people had none of the amenities that we have today. However, through sheer determination, faith in God, belief in themselves and each other, plus the will to succeed, they helped to make the country into what it is today. We could learn from them!

It is amazing that today, with all the creature comforts that we have, there is so much despair. Many think that the American dream is dead. Still others believe that the nation's golden years are behind. Sadly, the things that people once proudly recalled as part of their story are now seen as evidence of a system that is against them. A large segment of the populace no longer views challenges in their lives with the same perspective most once did. This in large part, is because of a prevalent political philosophy that continues to stir up dissatisfaction amongst the people.

Grievance is the tactic of choice, and proponents use every crisis as an opportunity to gin up the people against each other. Advocates of this philosophy tell the poor that it is the rich who are responsible for their poverty. They tell women that men are against them. They tell black people and minorities that white people want to subjugate them.

The proponents of the grievance culture have no problem destroying the characters of decent people. They call decent folk racist, misogynist, homophobes, and do whatever it takes to further their agenda. They are relentless. They are never satisfied.

Each night that you turn on your television set, one of them is pontificating about how terrible the country is. They assure us they have all the solutions. They tell us we just need to give them more power. They push the narrative that the only reason bad things happen to people is because others are working against them. They promise to fix all of the problems that ail us.

With them in power, they vow no one will ever have to worry about anything because they will prevent bad stuff from happening. Everything will be free. There will be no more poverty, no homelessness, no racism, no sickness or injustice. A law will be enacted to take care of every problem. Beware of them! With them in power, no one will ever again have a story to tell.

SOME THOUGHTS ON CLIMATE CHANGE

Greta And The Climate Doomsayers

Oh Greta! We knew it was true when you, as the 16-year-old doomsayer from Sweden had declared it to be the truth. These days Greta is hanging out at the United Nations scolding world leaders, and wagging her fingers at them.

Humanity would do well to pay attention to the teenager who had demonstrated that she knew what the heck she was talking about. She is a little older today, but when she speaks of the impending doom that is about to befall all of mankind, listen. She knows what she speaks of, and don't you forget it.

Be careful now! In order to validate her claims, she keeps flinging around the word science. Everyone knows that people are supposed to bow and do obeisance to the word "science" whenever some prominent person tosses it out. Make no mistake, lil Miss Greta is important.

So everyone, just listen to the teenage doomsayer, and cast off your ability to think. Cast aside your ability to read. Cast aside your ability to understand, to analyze and compare data, arguments, etc. The all-powerful word, "Science" renders anything that you think as useless. Deductive reasoning be damned! Inductive reasoning…psst…get outta here with that? Abductive reasoning what!?! SCIENCE!!!

So there you go. Beat that!

Having cleared that up (you're welcome), let's just agree with the former child prodigy, halo wearing kid from Sweden lecturing world leaders and citizens around the globe. If we do not stop using gasoline and other products that are derived from fossil fuels, we're all gonna die in…in…in 15 years, no in 25 years, make that…um…17 years. Okay, let's just continue ahead and play it safe…in one hundred years.

This child savant, now a young woman, wise beyond her years is undoubtedly humanity's last hope. We must listen to her! After all, the holy scriptures declare that "A child shall lead them." Ladies and gentlemen, people everywhere, here in America, and across the globe, THIS IS THE CHILD! (Albeit she's now older). And besides, Hollywood says she is the one. How's that for an added layer of certainty?

Mother earth has herself has sent Greta to bring the message to the world. The message is that we are all about to burn and die if we do not pay heed to her prophetic message. As she spreads her message of doom, her disciples demand that we all put aside our capacity to think. Like a bunch of sheep in need of a former child prodigy shepherd, just follow her lead.

Do not pay any attention to those false prophets who have come before her, declaring the end of the world. Forget that over the last six decades, not one of her predecessors has ever made one prophecy that has been fulfilled (and there have been many). She is the real deal! Pay attention to her. She knows what she is talking about.

The other doomsayers who predicted the end of the world in times past were also certain about their predictions of the perilous times ahead, but that's another story. They do not need to explain themselves to anyone. Just know that this time…this time…this time, the end really is nigh. If the world does not pay heed to the young know it all, Greta Thurnberg, it's over.

Yeah, yeah, yeah, everyone hears the protestations. But…but…but you say, what about the fact that Paul Erhlich predicted that millions upon millions upon millions would die of starvation by the 1970s or 1980s because of "overpopulation," and as a result the end of civilization would ensue? It don't matter!

Some remind that Dr David Viner, a senior research scientist at the climatic research unit (CRU) of the University of East Anglia said that "Within a few years winter snowfall will become a very rare and exciting event". Well, it depends on what within a few years means, but just in case anyone missed it the first time, here it is again for your benefit. It don't matter!

So what about when climate scientists said that if by the year 2000 the world did not get global warming (or was it climate change?) under control, it would be too late? That was then, this is now. It don't matter!

Did you not hear that 98 percent of scientists all over the world have formed a consensus that civilization is about to come to a cataclysmic halt? The earth as we know it will be destroyed in a cosmic vortex of CO2.

Oh oh, there's that word again…or at least a variation of it…scientists. Please throw all thinking out the window now! Thank you.

We all know that scientists are incapable of bias, right? They are pure as the wind-driven snow. They are incapable of promoting political agendas. Whatever they say goes, especially those scientists from that august body called the United Nations. No leftist agendas being driven from there, none whatsoever!

Most crucial though, Bill Nye says that we are all about to die if we don't stop driving SUVs. You know Bill Nye, right? Bill Nye is the "Science guy" who once upon a time used to hold to the stupid notion that boys are boys and girls are girls. Ok ok…must focus. That's a whole other issue.

Anyway, the thing is most Americans think it is imperative that we protect the environment. They want clean air and clean water. They don't want the forests to disappear, or the land to become a huge dump. That's why as a country, America has so many laws and mechanisms in place to protect the environment.

Americans are not against keeping the environment clean at all. They are just against environment worshippers who use the environment as an excuse for the government to make more and more laws that impose on people's freedom.

They are against using the environment to push political agendas.

They also do not buy in to the idea that the world is about to end because of climate change, because in the last 150 years of the earth's entire existence, the temperature has risen by .08 degrees.

Well, who cares? These stupid Americans are just a bunch of science/climate deniers anyway.

Let's Talk More Climate Change!

It's time to ask an important question! When people talk of climate change, what does that contrast with, in terms of the ideal? Is it climate constant?

Washington Post political correspondent Karen Tumulty once said in an interview that "Every fifth grader could tell you that climate change refers to unpredictable weather patterns." What she did not tell everyone is what the predictable patterns are that point to a normal climate. Let's go one step further and say that perhaps every third grader knows that climate change refers to unpredictable weather patterns. That still leaves a lot of unanswered questions concerning climate change.

Once upon a time, global warming was promulgated as the major threat to the world, then with no explanation, the danger switched from global warming to climate change. Today, climate change stands as the only field of scientific study that is not open to criticism or reexamination. I guess we can now add COVID-19 to the category of unquestionable science also, but that's another issue.

The science is settled they tell us. No dissenting voices are allowed. It does not matter what the credentials of anyone who questions the dogma of climate change as an existential threat to humanity and the earth may be. That person should be banished from the halls of academia, and the labs of scientific research. That individual is rendered as persona non grata for daring to question the certitude that humanity is in danger of extinction. That person is seen as scum's scum if he doubts that the world is about to be destroyed by climate change.

So let us circle back to the question asked earlier on, climate change as opposed to what, climate constant? If every modern day weather extreme that we experience is a sign that the world is about to end? The experts have to tell us what the specifics are of a climate that is not experiencing change, or a climate that is normal. How do citizens identify normal climate? What are the objectives of the goal we are working towards?

Instead of laying out broad vague terms like "fix the climate," or "get the climate under control," they have to tell the world what the standard is to determine if the climate has indeed been fixed after all of the recommended remedies are applied. What does a climate under control look like?

To be more specific, the experts will have to make everyone understand exactly how many hurricanes per year they consider as a sign of a climate under control. Will it be the same for the different locations around the world that do experience hurricanes? They will also have to let us know what the climate constant is for the number of hurricanes. They will have to let us know what the strength of hurricanes will be under a climate that is constant? What is acceptable for these factors during particular years?

But that is not all!

They will have to do the same thing and give specific numbers and details on tornadoes. They will have to do that for each state where these spectacular, dangerous wonders of nature take place every year. Beyond that, they will have to tell us what the acceptable margin of error is. That still will not be enough though. Someone will need to explain approximately what temperature range will be considered as normal during different times of the year. What exactly will be the acceptable constant temperature patterns in the summer months? How high should the temperature be during each month of the summer? Exactly how much seasonal overlap is acceptable with other months and seasons?

In the last few years, there has been some really unusual weather in the winter months, with some places across the U.S. experiencing some frigid weather. In other places, at other times, it has been unusually mild. If these weather phenomena indicate the scourge of climate change, then the climate pundits would need to articulate what the goal should be in terms of a climate that has been tamed. What is the constant that will show winters are no longer experiencing climate change?

It is not sufficient to say that the world needs to stop climate change. To reiterate the point, there must be clear indicators that will help to define a climate that is no longer changing. What are the specific barometers of a planet on the way to good health? These professionals will have to give the details for every state. As they collaborate with other countries, they will have to give us the details for every country. Based on their calculations, they will then have to let everyone know what the average climate for the world should be every year going forward.

After achieving the desired temperature range during the winter months, it will be important to highlight the amount of years that these patterns should continue before anything outside of the model is considered as just an aberration, and not a return to a state of climate distress.

For the unlearned, the ignorant, and the skeptical, these specifics are needed so that they would have a clear understanding of what a world free of climate change looks like. While the pros are at it, perhaps they will also explain the following details: How do we apply the experts' findings and measurements to droughts, floods, sea level, and the many other natural occurrences that are the result of adverse climate?

Tell the world exactly what the indicators of predictable weather patterns are so that there is no confusion. We need this information so that nothing would be left to chance, and people would know exactly what they are working to achieve.

The Weaponization Of The Word Science

Ever notice how people use the word science like a bludgeon to silence others? People get all haughty and they repeat the mantra, well we are just following the science. The science says X, or the science says Y, so shut up fool. Or they may say, I listen to the experts.

It's wise to follow the science. One should listen to the experts, but it's as though the word science or expert automatically negates another person's ability to think.

It does not matter how much garbage someone might be spewing in the name of science or expertise, everyone else is just supposed to listen and question nothing because, oooooohhhh the science.

The word science has now been elevated to God-like status. To question anything that some expert renders as science is now considered to be a conspiracy theory or, worse yet, blasphemy. People are afraid to question anything that is now called science for fear of being mocked, while others take on an air of sophistication when they utter the word, sticking their chin in the air, and twitching their head as they repeat the word: SCIENCE!

Dr. John Lennox is a brilliant man. He is Emeritus Professor of Mathematics at the University of Oxford, and an Emeritus Fellow in Mathematics and Philosophy of Science at Green Templeton College, Oxford University. He once made a very profound statement. He said that science does not tell us anything, scientists do. In other words, it takes human beings to look at science, interpret the data and determine what it says.

Do not think for one minute that scientists are robotic automatons in white cloaks, who operate like computers. They can only give you straight data without biases. If you believe that, you had better think again. These people are just as capable as any politician of cooking data to reflect their own biases, and they do. They don't get a pass simply because they throw out the word science to shut up anyone who challenges them.

No one would argue that gravity exists. We see gravity in action all around us every day. If the moon was further away or closer to the earth, it would have been catastrophic to life on earth. The sun is the right distance from the earth, so that it never gets too warm or too cold here, allowing life to flourish on earth. Those are scientific facts!

If however, the most brilliant physicist in the world was to spew nonsense, then in the words of Dr. John Lennox; "foolishness is foolishness even when spoken by brilliant scientists."

Dr. Lennox was referring to the influential, brilliant Stephen Hawking who once said "because there is a law of gravity the universe can create itself." It does not matter that Hawking was the world's premier physicist. His statement was a garbage statement on its face, and no one needed a degree in physics to know that.

People should stop genuflecting to the word science. No one should ever be afraid to challenge nonsense simply because someone utters the word science, or because a so-called expert says something that is obviously stupid. People must refuse to give up their capacity to think and analyze data.

Trust your doctor, but get a second and third opinion if you have doubts about something your doctor says. Sometimes it is necessary for people to do their own homework. Research, ask questions of the experts with differing opinions, then compare all the information and come to your own conclusion. This does not mean that one knows more than the experts, or that science is useless. Just do not cede your ability to think.

Never forget that scientists and experts are no different than other human beings, and they have often been wrong throughout history. How often has anyone ever heard the phrase "in a new study," or "the latest research has shown," then the statement moves on to contradict some long held idea that scientists/experts swore by before?

Scientists and experts can be just as ethically challenged, money can entice them. Like other human beings, the desire for adulation can compromise them. It's not only bankers, insurance salesmen, stockbrokers, lawyers or any of the regular suspects that people have been told to be suspicious of who are capable of deceit.

Sure professions are more prone to chicanery than others, but never think that so-called experts and scientists are always being straight when they put out their interpretations of data, or when they give you their computer models. Trust but verify also be applies to experts. One does not have to be intimidated by the word science.

Having said all of that, none of this means that you just go with what your neighbor Fitzroy or your aunt Gertrude has to say on a subject because either of them read a news article early one morning. Either of them hearing something on TV, or getting some information on a conspiracy website or podcast should not matter.

It is ok to trust the experts when they have shown themselves to be honest brokers, and earned the place of trust they hold. However, never ever be afraid of someone simply because they wear the tag of expert, or use the word science like a weapon. Do not give your mind over to anyone, whether that person be a cult leader, a dishonest expert, scientist or a quack.

LEFTIST POISON

The Brazen Leftward Tilt Of The U.S. Military

The military is becoming a leftist woke machine, and it is sad to observe. They are not completely gone as yet (they may almost be there), so there may still be a small window to summon Delta Force or Seal Team Six, to perform a rescue mission. It will be an extremely dangerous mission though, even for these formidable fighting forces.

When the left is in the ascendancy, they are difficult to defeat. They destroy everything in their path. Everything they touch turns to dirt.

As many look on in utter astonishment at the brazenly political posturing, and the embrace of leftist ideology by many in top leadership positions in the military, those who know the importance of the military remaining apolitical are becoming more and more concerned. The military must remain a politically neutral entity if the nation is to continue being a successful republic. If they do not, it is going to be a race to the bottom for the country. This will definitely bring an end to the United States' status as the most preeminent nation.

Those nations that have been nipping at our heels trying

o surpass the United States are waiting in the wings, ready to assume the role of the world's leading nation. For those who think that this is a good thing, how does it sound to have the brutal, despotic, communist nation of China calling the shots around the world? Yes, that China! The country that terrorizes its own citizens in slave camps, persecutes anyone who does not tow the political line, forces women to have abortions, is constantly haranguing its neighbors in the South China Sea, recently subjugated the people of Hong Kong, and unleashed a deadly virus on the world. That China!

Yup, that is the country that is lying in wait to usurp the role of the United States in the world. Right alongside them are our old friends, the Russians. Playing the lesser role as minions of these two powers are the Iranians and other bad actors who would no longer have to worry about the "evil" imperialistic U.S. of A.

This is what we face if the left continues to gain a foothold in the military. It will not happen overnight, but it will happen quicker than you know it.

Look at how swiftly their destructive prowess wreak havoc:

It is a safe bet that 10 years ago no one expected that there'd be serious discussions about whether a man could be a woman or a woman could be a man. No one thought people would be called bigots if they said that neither of these is possible. Did anyone think that in 2021, people would be called terrible human beings because they do not accept that men having sex with men or women having sex with women is a good thing?

Who would have thought that anyone would be hated, and that there would be calls to ostracize fellow citizens because they did not support gay marriage?

The left runs education, and large numbers of children are graduating high school unable to read and do math at grade level. Universities are hotbeds of intolerance for anyone who opposes leftist ideology.

Whereas sports was once a unifier, today no one can turn on a basketball game for respite from the constant bombardment of leftist ideology.

Once thriving cities like San Francisco are now havens for homelessness and drug addiction. Urban centers across America run by leftists are hotbeds for crime, poverty, and injustice.

The first amendment is under attack as people in power unabashedly declare their hostility against freedom of speech and freedom of religion.

As anti-police sentiment is now en vogue, we listen to calls to defund the police while murder and other violent crime continues to increase.

The Left Is Dangerous!

Given these examples of the left's destructive ways, what do we suppose will happen to the military if these people manage to firmly sink their claws into this organization, and implement their destructive policies? As they say, the proof of the pudding is in the eating.

All world powers eventually fall. It will not be any different for the United States. No one nation will be in the number one spot forever. Eventually, the day will come when the United States gives up its number one position in the world. That does not mean that Americans have to turn the military over to a bunch of crackpots. They do not have to watch the military become a place for leftist ideology, aiding in the country's decline. If this leftward shift of the military continues, it could hasten what would be a meteoric decline of a mighty nation.

Ultimately, in the grand scheme, almighty God has so much in store for the world. He will achieve his grand purpose as he weaves all the chaos in the world to produce the finest tapestry anyone can imagine. In the meantime though, Americans should not stand by in silence, nor retreat as they witness another institution embark on a course that leads to self-destruction.

The Poison of Leftist Ideology

Ladies and gentlemen, leftist ideology is a philosophy that is based on grievance. It relies on stirring up discontent among the people of the country in order to further leftist ideology. Now, to be clear, no one is saying that all the people on the left are malcontents who are trying to divide the people. At the core of this movement, facilitated by the movers and shakers of the ideology, is grievance. It is a pillar upon which much of the movement is built and continues to thrive.

Demons play a critical and necessary role in this philosophy. The left relies on the central role that demons play in order to be successful. Where veritable demons exist, the left must exaggerate the ramifications of their existence, and where none exists, the left has no problem pulling them out of thin air. They then go to work, feverishly trying to convince everyone that the world is on fire because of the demon on display. They then present themselves as the only ones with the hose and water to put out the fire they themselves started. This chicanery is often cloaked in the mantle of compassion in the effort to appeal to people's emotions.

Proponents of this sinister ideology care little about ideas because they are handicapped in the arena of ideas.

Let us take the topic of healthcare for one moment as an example of how they operate. Observe how the left is never ever willing to discuss healthcare in a dispassionate, rational way. Every attempt that conservatives make to fix the broken health care system, liberals immediately attack. They attack each attempt to restructure the system and make it workable. They say that any attempt to fix it is really an effort to leave people stranded in the wilderness. There the people will be surrounded by sickness, disease and a cabal of angry, evil white men whose only intent is to step on the downtrodden in order to feed an insatiable desire for riches.

They left has convinced people that health care is a need that they are entitled to which must be provided by the government. Any attempt to get people more invested in their own welfare must be based on evil intent, and an evil desire to fill the pockets of insurance companies or whoever the villain of the day may be.

Regardless of what one thinks of the issue, the point of this discussion is not about how to fix health care. The point is to emphasize the way that the left responds every time anyone makes efforts to correct the problem. They demonize their opponents, create an atmosphere of fear and stir up discontent.

One can observe the same approach to illegal immigration at any time. It is one of the most blatantly dishonest responses ever by the left on any topic. Those who are genuinely concerned about the overwhelming flow of none vetted people coming into the country illegally, and the possible consequences to our economy, our social welfare infrastructure, and our way of life, are labelled immediately as anti-immigrant. The issues that concerned Americans raise are summarily dismissed.

There is no interest by the left in having a serious discussion because maybe many of the issues that people raise will come across as legitimate. Once people have rational conversations, the left loses the advantage. Turning the discussion into accusations of hatred for immigrants, xenophobia and white supremacy keep the spirit of grievance alive. The left then gets to portray themselves as champions of the downtrodden in the make believe world that they create, all the while keeping the fires of discontent burning.

Another area that continues to be fodder for the grievance posse is abortion and birth control. There is absolutely no willingness by the people who call themselves progressive to discuss this sensitive issue honestly. Right out of the block, they frame the argument as "wanting to tell women what to do with their own bodies," when that is not at all what the issue is for most people who oppose abortion.

We will not get into a detailed discussion of abortion at this moment, but just for clarification; the issue is whether a woman should wantonly discard the life developing inside of her simply because nature made women the vessel through which life comes into the world. Does the barbarity of procedures like partial birth abortion belong in a civil society? Is it right that a twelve year old girl can walk into an abortion clinic and get an abortion without the approval of, or without notifying her parents?

On birth control, no one wants to ban it. It is absurd to suggest that anyone does. Many people simply have a problem with the government ordering businesses and insurance companies to provide contraceptives to anyone. People have a problem with forcing religious organizations to go against their conscience to provide abortifacient drugs simply because the government says that they must. They question why anyone else must pay for others' sex life.

The left is only interested in framing these arguments as a so-called war against women without ever addressing the nuances involved in all of these issues. Dealing with these matters in a calm, objective way is of no interest to them because it removes from their political arsenal, one of their chief weapons. Grievance!

These are not the only issues that they approach this way. Look at the way they have fomented hatred against the police. They have done this with devastating consequences to the communities that most need the police.

Observe as they continue to push the white supremacy narrative every day. They continue to cast aspersions on the white male with impunity. They push the narrative that America is a society that oppresses minorities and abuses its women.

If one disagrees with gay marriage, the left labels that person a homophobe. To be labeled transphobic, all you have to do is oppose the idea of men who call themselves women using women's bathrooms. If you point out the problem of Islamic terrorism, then you hate Moslems, and on and on it goes, with no end in sight what will offend them next.

For crying out loud, a person cannot even put on a sombrero for Cinco de Mayo. If that person is not Mexican, someone will accuse him of "cultural appropriation." The left is never satisfied no matter how much people try to appease them. Every time people buckle to their unreasonable demands, the left becomes more emboldened. It is time to say enough!

This is how these malcontents have operated for decades. Their tactics have been very successful, and they have made people afraid to open their mouths for fear of being tarred and feathered. Most people do not want to be labelled as racists. If someone successfully attaches the label, it can end friendships, divide families and destroy careers. Because of this, people cower in fear if their opinions are not in keeping with leftist doctrine. As a result, they avoid speaking out on the very important issues of race that matter to them.

Decent people do not want to be identified as hateful for simply having opinions that differ from the left. It is time however, to start standing up to this bully movement that is only interested in name calling, character assassination and pushing the grievance culture. Take it one step further, and say no to the one political party that has encouraged and been the aggressors of this poisonous movement.

Reject the Democrat Party!

Life On the Left As A Social Justice Warrior

Can you imagine living the life of a social justice warrior? Imagine that you draw every breath in a state of anger. The most meaningless words or gestures constantly offend you.

Every single morning, you wake up and you brace yourself for the battles that you think you must fight. Some of your biggest skirmishes are against words. You fight hard to eliminate these words from everyday usage. You spend every moment of your day in a state of readiness to do combat, because at any moment, some word could trigger you. This could then send you dashing for a safe space where you do not have to hear the offensive expression.

Often the words that offend are words that have been in use since the beginning of time. In the absence of a safe space to run to, a social justice warrior feels compelled to lash out at the perpetrator guilty of speaking the unapproved locution.

What must it be like to roam college campuses in search of forbidden opinions? How miserable must a person be trying to police the speech of others?

These are some of the most obnoxious, self-righteous people that you will ever come across in your life. They show up at private events with the express purpose of implementing the heckler's veto. They interrupt others from even discussing opposing points of view.

SJWs are constantly organizing protests and boycotts. One can only imagine how tedious it must be to live life denying basic truths like the fact that a man is a man, a woman is a woman, and neither can be the other. The pretenders then feign that they are truly offended because some do not share their views. To follow through on their denial, SJWs then resort to extremes to prove that they really believe the lies that they tell themselves every day.

Showing dedication to their cause, many social justice warriors willingly cut themselves off from their families who do not share their political views. Ruining a pleasant Thanksgiving or Christmas meal with their politics is not a problem for them. They will unfriend themselves on Facebook from someone they have known since childhood because the friend expressed solidarity with Trump or his policies. They then soak in their smugness with a feeling of superiority, convinced of their own virtue.

This bunch is always on the warpath. They are incapable of exercising the same tolerance that they demand of others. They are angry, hostile, petulant, offensive, aggressive, belligerent, insultive, and confrontational, even as they castigate others for daring to have an opinion that is different than their own. Their lack of self awareness is unparalleled, and they seem to think that their view of the world is the only outlook that matters. As far as they are concerned, they have the right, through the use of intimidatory tactics, to try and dissuade others from disagreeing with them.

One can only imagine that this must be a life that is absent of any joy or fulfillment.

Because almost everything offends the social justice warrior, they never have time to savor any of the blessings in their lives. This is because they always preoccupy themselves with the next battle. How tiresome must that be?

To those who don't live their lives preoccupied looking for things to be offended by, the life of a social justice warrior is soul destroying. Seemingly, the social justice warrior finds meaning in his misery. She is convinced that her cause is just, and perhaps it is that self-assured attitude above all that makes her dangerous.

Because SJWs regard themselves as the ultimate authority on what words mean, they can arbitrarily switch the meaning of words to mean whatever they want them to mean. When that happens, they can then justify their behavior in response to these words. In this world of "words are whatever I deem them to be" anything goes. They excoriate opponents for wrongdoing and no proof is ever necessary. They then justify their despicable behavior by convincing themselves they are fighting evil. Feeling justified, they wage unrelenting efforts to end people's careers. They shame some, ostracize others, physically try to intimidate yet more, and even violently attack people whose only crime is that they said something offensive or hold the wrong political opinion.

Left to continue their campaign of self-righteousness, the only thing they will leave in their wake is a trail of brokenness and destruction.

Do not let them continue unchallenged.

Socialism "Wins" Every Time

In the world of every Socialist die hard loyalist, no one would have a story of overcoming difficulty to relate, because the government will always be right there to jump in to the rescue. In that world, the government should make everything all right. No one could give any examples of how hard work in the face of difficulty pays off for anyone. People will not be able to demonstrate that fighting to overcome unfavorable circumstances builds character, or how battling obstacles can lead to innovation.

You see, in the mind of socialists like the esteemed Congress woman Alexandria Ocasio Cortez, no one should ever have to go through difficulties in life. So, for example; if you are a college student working two jobs to help you make it through school, and you have periods when you could only afford to eat ramen soup, that is not considered as paying your dues, and helping you to deal with the tough issues that life sometimes throw in your way.

In the world of people like the august Congresswoman, that is the result of an unfair system that is designed to only benefit the rich, and take advantage of the less fortunate. You see, for socialists, in life, when horrific things happen, it is always someone else's fault. Awful things never happen because sometimes that is just the way life is. It's not that people may learn to be responsible, to be frugal, discreet, productive or any of the reasons that we have traditionally been taught.

Alexandria Ocasio Cortez and her ilk will have none of that. In their utopian world, no one should have problems because uncle government is always right there to take them all away.

People do not have to invest in their own future by making sacrifices. People do not need to delay self-gratification, spend their own money on things like education, health care, housing and other life necessities. They do not simply need to learn to improve their own lives. The philosophy of Ms. Cortez is that no one should ever know what it is to be broke, or struggle to meet their monthly obligations.

Are you having problems paying your rent? That is just unfair. Got no money to fill your tank up with gas? No one should ever have to experience that. No money in the bank to get you out of a jam or emergency? That should never, ever have to happen to anyone because in the socialist world of Alexandria Ocasio Cortez and her other comrades, bad things simply should not happen to people. She will ensure that people never have to go through any of these life challenges in the future again.

Free health care for all, free college education, free housing. Whatever you need, whatever ails you, Alexandria Ocasio Cortez will fix it for you. She will see that the rich provide it for you, because everyone knows that taking from the rich to give to give to the poor is the one sure way to grow an economy, right? That's how the rich got to be rich in the first place, isn't it? Somebody gave them their riches. Steve Jobs, Bill Gates, Warren Buffet, Steve Forbes, Mark Zuckerberg, Jack Dorsey, and all of these millionaires and billionaires as Bernie Sanders so derisively likes to talk about them, are all crooks. They all got to be rich by stealing from the poor, not on the strength of their ideas, nor the goods and services they provide. And besides, they never went through hardships getting to where they are.

Mark Zuckerberg just woke up one morning, came up with Facebook, presented it to the world the next day, then ta-daaa. He was rich. Steve Jobs did the same with Apple, and Bill Gates never had to deal with any obstacles coming up with Microsoft. Those oil barons never had to take risks, work hard, experience sleepless nights or wonder how they would meet their obligations. They all just woke up one day, and voila; they were all very rich. Therefore, it is no big thing for the Government to come in, and just take the fruits of everyone's labor. Uncle Govvy could then distribute it as he sees fit, to eliminate the problems and the struggles of the less fortunate. Those rich people did not earn it.

We know that when life is easy for everyone, and there are no major obstacles to overcome, that brings out the spirit of innovation in people. That is when human beings are at their absolute best, right?

So let's cheer for Alexander Ocasio Cortez, Bernie Sanders, and all the other Socialists in the Democrat Party. We know that in the past, their policies have been successful through-and-through wherever they have been tried. Who needs to teach men to fish when you can simply take fish from the rich and give them to all those in need? What a remedy for success!

Life will never ever be difficult again for anyone. No one will have to struggle. No one will ever be poor again. The rich are about to get their comeuppance because Alexander Ocasio Cortez will take 70 percent of what they have rightfully earned through their own efforts, and the sweat of their own brows. She wants to then give it to those who are "more deserving."

So far, she has been unsuccessful with all of her goals. Just give her party some more power.

Hopefully, her redistribution efforts will include taking from people like her fellow socialist Bernie Sanders and others in the Democrat Party who have gotten supremely rich off the teat of government. After all Bernie does not need those three houses that he owns. Take at least one and give it to a family that needs it more than he does.

Here is to the success of socialism everyone!

Hip hip…

Do Not Forget Who The Left Is

As the self-righteous left continues to pontificate and paint themselves as the salt of the earth, do not forget who these people are. These same people who continue to talk about a bunch of unarmed thugs who stormed the Capitol as insurrectionists are the same people who appealed to violence repeatedly during the Trump Presidency. Violence was a staple that they used in their resistance to Trump.

Do not forget it, violence and intimidation were staples, and breaking all the political norms that are usually afforded a President went out the window with Donald Trump. This all happened just four years ago to the Trump's Presidential inauguration. It is too early for revisionism.

Leading up to President Trump's inauguration, it was no lesser figure than the race pimp John Lewis who called Trump an illegitimate President. He and 66 other members of Congress refused to attend President Trump's inauguration. Maxine Waters said that she would never work with him on any issue. Before Trump even took office, she talked of impeaching him...before he even took office.

Don't forget that during Trump's inauguration leftist mobs raged and rioted on the streets of Washington D.C. They smashed cars, and store fronts. They got in violent confrontations with the police. They set cars on fire, and damaged police vehicles. Who can forget the dramatic picture of a stretch limo that was set on fire by the marauding hordes of protestors? By the time it was over the police had arrested over 200 agitators.

The mob did not restrict their actions to Washington D.C. though, they took their protests to cities across America during the inauguration. How about when on the day after the inauguration, leftist agitators shouted "not my President?" They blocked highways and other roadways, and in Portland they even caused the delay of trains.

After Trump was inaugurated the FBI put out information to the media about a supposed dossier that showed Trump paid prostitutes to pee on a bed on which Obama had slept, then based on absolutely nothing they launched a three year attack accusing Trump of being a Russian stooge.

Democrats and the leftist news media proceeded to call Trump all sorts of names. Even former spy chiefs James Clapper and Paul Brennan were all over the airwaves, suggesting and saying that Trump is a Russian asset. For the entire four years that Trump was President they never let up from their attacks. To this day Hillary Clinton continues to refer to Trump's tenure as President as illegitimate.

We had Maxine Waters encouraging people to get aggressive and harass members of Trump's team in gas stations, theaters, and supermarkets. Wearing a MAGA hat became a potential hazard to the wearer. Celebrities were on Twitter and all over the media competing to see who could attack Trump in the most vile manner. Many openly spoke of how delighted they would be if he died a violent death.

The Democrats in the Senate held up Trump's cabinet nominations, though in fairness, Obama's nominations also took a long time to be approved. The Democrats did everything in their power to sabotage Trump's every move. They could not even rejoice when he killed two of the most violent terrorists responsible for the deaths of Americans across the globe. Even that was an occasion for them to criticize Trump.

They called Trump every nasty name in the book. For the entire four years of his Presidency, Tump was unable to find any cooperation from the Democrat Party. They railed, and they railed, and they railed against him down to his last days.

They impeached him for asking the leader of Ukraine to "interfere in the Presidential election." There was nothing in the transcript of Trump's call with the Ukrainian President that showed any such request. There was literally no discussion about the elections in the call that the Democrats accused him of making, but that's not all.

In a hurried manner, they impeached Trump for purportedly inciting an insurrection, without affording him any opportunity to defend himself. This happened over the period of a few days.

No one could produce any video, audio or any evidence of Trump inciting the so called insurrection, but that did not matter. Dirtying up Trump on his way out as much as they could was the goal.

This is not even a quarter of the story. Make sure to remember all of this. Don't be vindictive. Do not resort to their tactics, but certainly do not play by their rules.

These are the people who would lecture the deplorable. Pay these hypocrites no mind.

The Righteous Violence And Sinister Tactics Of the Left

Once again, the left and the Democrat Party machine are shouting to anyone who would listen that their violence is better than everyone else's violence. Their violence is justified, everyone else's violence is not. They have reason to loot, burn, vandalize and just tear stuff apart. Others don't even have reason to protest.

The handful of people who resort to violence from time to time on the other side are then used to portray a whole movement as vile white supremacists.

Because of an act of stupidity and lawlessness on 6 January by a few people, the media and the left have shamelessly used the incident to portray it as the norm on the right. They have done so knowing it's not true. It is anything but the norm on the other side.

The legacy media have falsely labeled what happened on 6 January an insurrection. Sure, there was no excuse for what occurred on the U.S. Capitol that day. That it was an insurrection is ridiculous. The actions of the rioters cannot be justified. They deserve the harshest condemnation. Those who took part should face the consequences of their actions. Everyone who played any role in what happened should pay the penalty for what they did.

The media would have us believe ANTIFA played no role in anything that happened. They quickly dismiss any mention of ANTIFA. None of the so-called journalists who are supposed to bring us the impartial news have any interest in even looking in to the role that ANTIFA may have played. They are not interested in digging deeper. They could not care any less about doing the investigative work that journalist were once so proud to do to get to the bottom of any story.

Now journalists simply depend on the noise that is concentrated in their own bubble for any information on varying subjects. That we have heard nothing about any role the left may have played inciting and taking part in the violence speaks volumes. The legacy media have refused to feature anything on the role that John Sullivan, the radical leftist Antifa agitator played in the 6 January riots.

Despite there being lots of information that shows him advocating the use of violence in his efforts to get rid of Trump, they underplay his role in J6. There is video of him calling on his supporters to burn sh** down and members on his chat group boasting how they disguised themselves as Trump supporters as part of their strategy to cause chaos on 6 January 2021 at the U.S. Capitol.

This does not mean that there were no unruly Trump supporters on 6 January 2021. It's just that we know subterfuge and violence are mainstays of the left. There are other videos online that show the role the left played instigating and participating in the violence of that day.

The media's silence on this matter is stunning. If it weren't for alternate media like Breitbart, The Gateway Pundit, The Daily Caller, OAN, and others, nobody would know about this because of the media's silence. Trump's supporters definitely participated in the mayhem on that regrettable day, no doubt about it. We cannot pretend that they are innocent. They are not, but to what extent can the events of that day can be blamed on them?

The idea that hundreds of thousands of people who showed up that day were rabid white supremacists, intent on causing violence and overthrowing the government is a lie. Innocent people whose only crime was protesting what they saw as a fraudulent election are now sitting in jails as political prisoners. Some of the protestors have been rotting in jails without bail for trespassing on the Capitol. There is even video that shows Capitol police removed barriers, and let people onto the compound as part of the effort to instigate the bedlam.

Any information that moves away from the narrative that Trump's supporters were not the only ones responsible for the shameful events of that day is dismissed. They casually disregard the people who attempt to draw attention to the role that the left played as conspiracy theorists.

We saw another version of the left's 6 January tactics during the rise and subsequent struggle of the Tea Party movement.

Leftists would infiltrate Tea Party rallies with signs, and engaged in despicable behavior in the effort to paint Tea Party members as racists, misogynists, homophobes etc.

It was so well documented that Tea Party members were always ready to capture and expose them on video. We even have a more recent example of this venomous behavior by the left, during the recent Virginia elections. A small group of candidate McAuliff supporters showed up with tiki torches pretending to be white supremacist supporters of now governor-elect Glen Youngkin.

The point of rehashing all of this is to remind people of the danger that the left poses. They are evil from the inside out. They are evil all the way from the soles of their feet to the top of their heads. Their outright wickedness is never given the coverage that it earns and deserves from the dishonest media. This is not to excuse the right and Trump's supporters for their part in the January 6 pandemonium. Far from it.

This is just to show the difference in the way the right and the left gets covered. This is to show that the left can do no wrong. The media will do everything to cover for them. The left will not be called to account for their despicable deeds how the right is called to account when they do wrong.

Make no mistake. The handful of people who were involved in the mayhem and violence on 6 January deserve the penalty that their actions call for, all of them, including the Antifa actors. Observe however, right now; as the left does what they do best, they are wreaking havoc all over Democrat cities. They are running amok, beserking, causing all kinds of tumult, and dishing out violence.

The media and the Democrat machine does not show the same outrage. A black nationalist recently used his vehicle to kill as many people as he could with his vehicle in Waukesha Wisconsin. A review of his Facebook page revealed he has called for violence against white people and espoused some of the most detestable anti police, anti-Jewish and other extreme views imaginable. No matter though, leftist violence is righteous violence.

The madness we are currently witnessing all over the country right now is just a continuation of what we saw in 2020 when the left used the unfortunate killing of a black man to push a false narrative. They used this man's death to justify their chaos. They rioted in cities across America for over 180 days straight, as the legacy media refused to cover the violence. We had Kamala Harris and other high-profile people on the left paying the bail of many rioters, while prosecutors refused to file charges against many of the violent perpetrators.

The media looked on, as night after night, people attacked federal buildings and tried to burn them down. We looked on in disbelief as the media made every excuse in the book for rioters. On the other hand they could only muster the courage to condemn President Trump for sending federal officers to protect the federal buildings.

Call this what it is.

This is evil!

No Entity Lies And Wages War On The Truth Like The American Mainstream Media And The Left

The new model of the left is not just to spread propaganda, but they have zoned in on portraying the truth as lies and lies as truth. This is evil like we have not seen in the United States before. Make no mistake, lies and propaganda have always been around, but in the United States there has always been an emphasis on Judaeo Christian values that emphasize the importance of truth.

Unlike many nations before, the United States emphasizes truth. Not that the United States is perfect, in fact, far from it. Like individuals, no country is flawless. The United States certainly is not. The United States though, has always been a nation of laws and a nation that values truth. Even if the country never fully achieves it because we live in an imperfect world, truth is an American value.

The attacks on truth by the left and the media in the current day United States are brazen and evil. These people are not even trying to hide their deception. It is a two pronged attack of propaganda where they spread lies in the effort to push an evil agenda. Even worse is the attacks on truth. Don't believe your lying eyes says the media. Pay no attention to your untruthful ears. It is we who are telling the truth says the lying media and the left.

What is most insane though is that the lies they tell are big lies, huge, gargantuan lies that are obvious lies.

Recently, they launched a rampage against podcaster Joe Rogan in their continued COVID-19 misinformation campaign.

They did not like that Rogan's doctor recommended Ivermectin to fight the virus. It is because they have totally sold out to pushing vaccines and discouraging any other treatment of the virus.

In what seemed like a coordinated effort after Rogan talked about his use of Ivermectin, all the major media houses claimed Ivermectin is a horse dewormer. They then claimed that hospitals were being overwhelmed by people needing treatment for Ivermectin overdoses. It got so bad that one hospital had to come out and give a statement correcting the media misinformation. They said they did not treat one patient for Ivermectin overdose.

It truly was an awful display of media malpractice. Despite the temptation to label their shameless exhibition of media misinformation as shocking, regrettably, it was not. It is now a very familiar occurrence. For those of us who have been observing these charlatans for years, this was nothing new. We have seen even scarier things.

In the wake of the last elections, the media incessantly repeated the mantra that there was no evidence of fraud or irregularities? They continue to say it even now, even as more and more evidence comes out that there was definitely election fraud. Not that they are claiming the evidence for election fraud is weak. They did not say that it is too late after the elections to raise all of these issues. They are not saying that the case for fraud has too many holes. They are not presenting counter arguments. They are telling everyone that there is no evidence…none.

These are the same people who told us that Trump is a Russian Spy. Vladimir Putin compromised him. Keep in mind the only time the Robert Mueller investigation team made any public comment during the whole Russia investigation fiasco was to correct media misinformation.

These people told us that the protests we saw during the summer of 2020 were mostly peaceful. They told us this as all across the country we witnessed burning cities, rioting, looting, mayhem and murder. Just as sinister as their attacks on truth, and the spreading of propaganda, is what they withhold from the public. The media refused to speak the truth about Michael Flynn and what really happened to him. They celebrated over this patriot being a political target of the FBI, and the media continues refusing to highlight the corruption of the judge who oversaw his case. The torrent of violence against supporters of Donald Trump never did matter to our betters in the media. As people were attacked for wearing MAGA hats, the media could not care less. They have no interest in stories like these because they run against the set narrative.

They made excuses for Joe Biden even when we saw with our own eyes and heard with our own ears Joe Biden boast that he threatened to withhold aid from Ukraine if that government did not fire a prosecutor he did not like.

We read the transcript with our own eyes of Trump's conversation with the Ukraine President. Yet despite what we heard with our own ears, the Democrats, protected by the media, told us Trump asked the President of Ukraine to interfere in the presidential elections. Then in the weeks leading up to the elections, as stories of corruption broke about Biden family corruption, the media told us it was

Russian disinformation, only now to admit that it was true after all. The media smeared anyone who dared attempt to get out the story.

The lying liars who love to lie while lying as they lie told us that Trump advised Americans to drink bleach and inject disinfectant into their systems to fight the Corona virus. They still repeat this lie with a straight face. They told us, and continue to tell us up to this day, that Trump said there are good Nazis. Not one reporter ever dares to interrupt Joe Biden whenever he repeats that lie to say the former President never said that. This is despite anyone being able to go on to YouTube or other streaming service and view videos of what Trump actually said, but it does not matter.

They told us that Trump called the Corona virus a hoax when they know that he never did that. All you have to do is look at what he said during the rally when he used the word hoax regarding the Corona virus, and you would see that he was attacking the Democrats' attempts to politicize the Corona Virus. He called what they were doing a hoax, but none of that matters. Don't believe your lying eyes and your untruthful ears.

There are many more stories like this. It is now a pattern of behavior by the media to engage in outright lies, propaganda, and flagrantly attacking the truth. The fake news media in this country is the enemy of the people.

IS THE DEMOCRAT PARTY A HATE GROUP?

Confronting The Democrat Party's History Of Hate

First, it is critical to state up front that no one here has any delusions that the Republican Party is saintly. No one is saying that conservatives do not have undesirables in their movement. Far from it, human beings are badly flawed. The sinful nature is dominant in all of us. It takes a concentrated effort, and a willingness to fight the demons that plague us all to overcome these demons. In addition, it takes the grace of Almighty God to combat and overcome our human frailties. The Republican Party and those on the right are no different. Having made that point, it is interesting to note that the media, and advocates of the left constantly make excuses for the recalcitrant behavior that is firmly rooted on the left. On the other hand, those on the right are held to a completely different standard.

The Democratic Party and Democrats in general, from the inception of their party, have been responsible for almost every atrocity, and inhumane law or policy ever committed or passed in the country. From slavery to the trail of tears, lynchings, Jim Crowe, Segregation, forced sterilizations, pushing eugenics philosophy, internment of the Japanese and other ethnic groups, the Ocoee massacre, the Rosewood massacre, the black Wall Street massacre, and the dreaded prison gangs of the South known as peonage, which some have described as worse than slavery. These are all the legacy of Democrats.

This is the party that opposed reconstruction, the Freedmen's Bureau Act, gave rise to the Klu Klux Klan, and opposed the thirteenth, fourteenth, fifteenth and nineteenth amendments. Every major opposition to civil rights legislation from the eighteen sixties to the height of the civil rights movement received the most opposition from the Democrat Party. Republican efforts successfully diminished the Klu Klux Klan's influence, only for the group to be revitalized in the 1920s after a Democratic President showcased "Birth of a Nation" at the White House. The Klan then once again became the terroristic arm or the Democratic Party, unleashing a reign of terror on blacks all across America.

Democrats opposed the Civil Rights Act of the eighteen sixties, The Civil Rights Act of 1957, and the Civil Rights Act of 1960. By the time their party finally came around to supporting the civil rights act of 1964, members in their party tried to filibuster the bill. They even opposed the nomination of the first black man nominated to the Supreme Court.

Republicans in Congress continued to lead the way with all the subsequent civil rights legislation of that era. The left points fingers at Barry Goldwater for opposing the nineteen sixty-four legislation as proof of the Republican Party opposition to civil rights. The truth is Barry Goldwater was a civil rights leader before it became popular. He was in favor of civil rights advancement and did a lot to advance the cause of civil rights prior to the civil rights bill of nineteen 1964.

Goldwater promoted civil rights in the state of Arizona and played a vital role in helping to bring the goal of equality closer for blacks in his state. He even integrated the Arizona National Guard when he was governor of Arizona, before Harry Truman dreamt of doing it with the rest of the military. Even though Truman signed the executive order integrating the military, it was only rigorously enforced during the Eisenhower Administration.

The only reason that Barry Goldwater opposed the civil rights act of 1964 was because of provisions in the bill that he felt gave too much power to the Federal Government and took too much from the States. He wanted changes to the bill to avoid that. Today, with the Federal Government reigning supreme, and the states losing more and more of their autonomy, his concerns now seem like they were prescient.

The Democrat Party once boasted hundreds of thousands of Klansmen. Currently, the Klan is a toothless tiger with less than ten thousand members across the country. They have scant to no influence. Despite their diminished influence and dwindling membership, the media relentlessly tries to portray the Klan as a powerful movement. This is all done in the effort to try to link the present day Klan with the Republican party, and the conservative movement. No such link has ever existed. If one belongs to the Klan, that person is not allowed to join, and cannot be a member of the Republican Party.

Democrat legislatures passed every segregationist law ever enacted in America, and Democrat governors signed them. To reiterate, there is not a single piece of segregationist legislation that was ever passed by a Republican legislature or signed by a Republican governor. In addition, the next time anyone looks at a video of innocent, peaceful black marchers being set upon by dogs, remember that the man by the name of Bull Connor responsible for that act was a Democrat.

The Democrats have never apologized for their sordid past. However, to redeem themselves, they simply claim that contrary to everything we know about human nature, "The big switch" took place after the civil rights movement. They say that all the Democrat segregationists switched parties.

Democrats became the party of civil rights, and the Republicans became the party against civil rights. In other words, the party that was responsible for so much atrocities, and wreaked so much terror on Americans for over one hundred and fifty years, just suddenly had an epiphany, and changed their ways. Then the party that was formed to lead the fight for, and spearheaded the cause of civil rights during the same time just switched places. The bad guys became the good guys, and the good guys became the bad guys. The police became the robbers, and the robbers became the police. It is a lie! It never happened. How such a story could ever have taken root is difficult to understand.

The next time someone says that the parties switched, all

one has to do is ask the person who the Dixiecrats are that switched. What were their names and how many of them there were? If the person tries to switch the topic to the South turning Republican, just remind that individual that the South never turned Republican until the nineties.

Today all the Democrats have to do is claim that anyone who does not embrace their socialist agenda, or their controversial policies is a racist, misogynist, sexist, xenophobe, islamophobe or a homophobe. They do that and all of their past is forgiven by Hollywood, academia, the media and corporate America. That remains enough for them to continue getting a pass. It is absolutely fascinating to observe, but that is not all.

As already noted, the left and the Democratic Party also have an absolutely horrible history of political violence. While the media, and other defenders of the left become ecstatic, and jump for joy at every opportunity to point out violent behavior on the right, they ignore the violence that is an intrinsic part of leftist ideology.

The left justifies violence in the name of "the struggle." They rejoice and dance on the graves of victims when they get to point a finger at Dylan Roof as an example of violence on the right. Dylan Roof belonged to no recognized conservative group, and acted on his own accord but that does not matter.

By the same token, the left remained silent when a man linked to the Black Lives Matter Movement committed a massacre against the police. He killed five Police Officers in cold blood all in the name of "justice" for black men. When a Hilary Clinton supporter committed the atrocious Orlando night club shooting, killing over fifty people and injuring over two hundred, the media refused to highlight the Hillary Clinton link.

Let's be frank, although Hillary Clinton had nothing to do with his committing the unspeakable act, we must ask the question. What justifies the double standard in the response to what he did? Why the attempt to link Roof's act of violence to conservative ideology, but none to link the Orlando shooter's act to leftist ideology? Why the double standard when a black man shouting Allahu Akbar, targeting white men on the streets of Los Angeles killed three people in his attack?

Why was it not newsworthy when a black man, in response to "police brutality against black men," set off one of the biggest structural fires in the history of Los Angeles, destroying several buildings, causing excessive pollution and costing the City tens of millions of dollars? It is quite significant that if you do an online search you will not find information on this arson that was committed in Los Angeles about five years ago.

Just to mention one more time, no one is claiming that the right is guiltless or that they have not committed violence. However, violence as a tactic is a pillar of the left. Vitriol is its close ally. People have to continue calling out this movement for its bullying tactics. This bullying can be seen across the decades in even more examples. It can be seen in the absolutely wild response to Donald Trump's election as President of the United States.

It is the left that supports and rallies for people like the murderers Mumia Abu Jamal, and Asata Shakur, two cop killers. It is the left who lauds the freed terrorist Óscar López

Rivera, whose organization was responsible for several bombings all across America, killing five innocent people in the process.

The left shamelessly walks around with images of the psychotic, deceased maniacal, bloodthirsty zealot Che Guevara emblazoned across the front of their T-shirts. Guevara had no redeeming quality. Everyone knows about his penchant for sadistic brutality and dislike of black people, but the left adores him. The Una bomber was a disciple of left-wing ideology. The assassins of President Kennedy, President McKinley and President Lincoln were on the left, Democrats, or sympathizers. It is a leftist who made an attempt on the life of Franklin D. Roosevelt. Two leftist women attempted to kill President Ford.

In 2011 a young man from the Occupy Wall Street movement fired a bullet at the white house during President Obama's tenure. Do not forget that during the 2016 election, Donald Trump was the only candidate who was attacked on the stage by a supporter of the other candidate. In town hall meetings after Trump's election, it is only Republican members of congress who were attacked by leftist protesters showing up at the gatherings.

The destructiveness of leftist ideology can be seen across the world, from the shores of present day Venezuela (a once prosperous nation) to the plains of Zimbabwe, stretching all the way back to Stalinist Russia, the people's revolution of China, the jungles of Vietnam, the killing fields of Cambodia, working its way all across the Oceans back to Cuba, and traversing much of Latin America. There are not too many success stories, but tens of millions of dead bodies as a direct result of leftist violence.

Despite almost successful attempts to rewrite history, Hitler's Germany is another glaring example of the left's ability to descend into the pit of ruthlessness. Yes folks, you read that right, Nazism as practiced by Hitler, and his party was another brand of leftist ideology, but do not believe anything written here. Go examine the 25 planks of Hitler's "Nazionalsocialist" Party and his speeches, and you will see that it reads like anything you would hear at the Democrat Party Convention.

As much as the left likes to call conservatives anti-Semitic, it is they who constantly engage in blatant anti-Semitism. The BDS movement is a product of the left. Anti-Semitism across college campuses is a commodity of the left. Rashida Tlaib, Ihlan Omar, Alexandria Ocasio Cortez and their brand of antisemitism is a product of the left. To be clear again, it is not that the right is blameless and there is no anti-Semitism on the right.

The main point being made is that the left is responsible for the majority of anti-Semitism in the country. It was not the right who was engaging in the knockout game a few years ago, while the leftist propaganda media machine told the rest of the country that the knockout game was another conspiracy theory conjured up by the right.

The left attempts to link conservatives and the Republican Party to Nazis because of the Republican Party's stance on illegal immigration, and their America first stance. Hitler's platform had nothing to do with illegal immigration, low taxes, welfare reform, or the efficiency of capitalism, free market reform of the health insurance industry, or anything espoused by conservatives.

The Nazis' treatment of the Jews had more in common with the way Democrats treated blacks in America. It had nothing to do with how the Republican Party has ever treated any group of people. The Nazi college leaders burned books to stifle speech, and anything they considered wrong think. It is the left who engages in that behavior right here and now.

Today the left riots, uses the heckler's veto, and other forms of intimidatory tactics to keep those they disagree with from speaking on university campuses across the country. Violence against conservative speakers is a major threat. It is to where conservative speakers must have intense personal security when they give speeches at universities. The left independently declares these speakers to be hate mongers who must be silenced using any means necessary.

The Democrat Party has been on the wrong side of every major issue this country has faced. Today, they continue to use race to divide people, albeit with a new twist. Today they attack the white male in a sick and twisted attempt to compensate for their history of injustice against blacks. In addition, they continue to use Government programs to lure black people to their party. They hope to keep black people dependent on Government in order to secure the votes of blacks.

This tactic of giving black people stuff started way back in the nineteen thirties. During this period, the Democrats denied blacks the benefits that they extended to whites during the Great Depression. They always gave them just enough to keep them quiet. They gave them just enough to keep them coming back, while denying them genuine opportunities to be successful full-fledged Americans. The left's reign of terror against blacks continued unabated.

Despite their treatment of black citizens, they began securing the black vote by feeding black people scraps to keep them dependent on Government. Not withstanding the Democrats' awful history of terror against blacks, and despite the lack of economic progress for many black Americans, blacks became more and more dependent on them.

That continues to this day. They tell black people that those who oppose the policies of the left want nothing but to take their stuff away. They convinced many black people that the scraps the Government feeds them is divine sustenance from their benevolent benefactors, the Democrats.

As one prominent commentator so eloquently put it, the "Democrat Party has persuaded many black people to think that clinging to a rope while those at the top try to pull them up is better than providing those at the bottom with a ladder to climb to the top."

The ladder is risky, and maybe those climbing it may fall. Sometimes they may need the help of others to hold the ladder a bit, but making it to the top will mostly depend on their own effort. Some will not make it, but those who cling to the rope while someone attempts to pull them up are at the complete mercy of the person pulling up the rope.

Today in places like Baltimore, Los Angeles, Philadelphia, Ferguson, Detroit, Chicago and other cities all across America run by Democrats, too many black people and other minorities are clinging to the rope. They are desperately reaching for scraps while they hang on for dear life. Many of these people will continue to vote for the Democrat Party because they are convinced that those who offer them another way, leading to the path of self-reliance, are racists.

Here are a few examples of Democratic race baiting using white people as the bait from the headlines of established media outlets over the last few years. In a strange twist, they even claim that some black people are white supremacists:

Brittney Cooper, a Rutgers' professor: "I think white people are committed to being villains in the aggregate, right? The real sort of issue here and I've heard people sort of say it is, one I think that white people sort of viscerally fear, it's not that white people don't know right, what they have done. They know. They fear that there is no other way to be human, but the way in which they are human which is…so you know that whenever you talk to white people and you wanna have a reckoning about it they say stuff like, you know it's just human nature. If yall had all of this power, you would have done the same thing, right? And it's like, no that's what white humans did. White humans thought there's a world here and we own it. Prior to them black and brown people have been sailing across oceans interacting with each other for centuries without total subjugation, domination and colonialism.

Los Angeles Times: Larry Elder (a black man who ran for Governor of California) is the new face of white supremacy according to the LA Times: you've been warned.

Psychiatrist speaking at Yale tells the audience she fantasizes about shooting white people in the head.

Salon: White Men Must be stopped: The very future of mankind depends on it.

Children's book author Meena Harris: violent white men are the greatest terrorists in our country.

Lena Dunham: celebrates "the extinction of white men."

Drexel Professor: calls for a white Genocide.

Chelsea Handler: Stacy Dash and Ben Carson are "black white supremacists."

Wisconsin College Democrat leader closely affiliated with the Clinton 2016 presidential campaign: resigned after tweeting "I f—ing hate white men."

A New York Times Columnist and professor at Yeshiva University: wrote an op-ed stating that he'll be raising his children to not trust white people.

Who can forget the black female professor Said Grundy who famously said "White masculinity isn't a problem for America's colleges, white masculinity is THE problem for America's colleges," she also said "Every MLK week I commit myself to not spending a dime in white-owned businesses. And every year I find it nearly impossible."

Check out the words of a Trinity College Professor by the name of Eric Williams in response to representative Steve Scalise's shooting that was committed by a Bernie Sanders supporter: "It is past time for the racially oppressed to do what people who believe themselves to be 'white' will not do, put an end to the vectors of their destructive mythology of whiteness and their white supremacy system."

What is most alarming is that these are not random trolls that you can find on all sides of the political divide. These are prominent people on the left who continually spew this kind of rhetoric. The irony is that they will look to the people who highlight their behavior and accuse those who call them out of being racist.

Just for the heck of it, let's look at another example of this white hatred that has been on display for a few years and is becoming more brazen. This is from a Black Lives Matter affiliated group called F Yo Flag. This is from their radio show a few years ago. A man called in to the show, and went on a hatred filled racist rant, calling for violence against white people as the host agreed with him.

This is what the caller said: "When those mother f**kers are by themselves, that's when we should start f***ing them up. Like they do us, when a bunch of them ni**ers takin' one of us out, that's how we should roll up." He said, "Cause we already roll up in gangs anyway. There should be six or seven black mother f**ckers, see that white person, and then lynch their a**. Let's turn the tables."

This is the kind of stuff that is now praised as being "woke," or "brave," "unafraid to speak truth to power," and "telling it like it is." Ladies and gentlemen, it is none of these things. It is just dangerous! No doubt there are lots of decent people on the left, but the machine that continues to spread the horrific bilge on the left must be combatted fearlessly by those who do not wish to see the country continue down this road.

Stand up to this divisiveness. Make no mistake about it, the left will insult, call names and resort to all kinds of intimidatory tactics to silence anyone who opposes their behavior. Stand up to them anyway!

The Democrat Party Rage Machine

Someone on the radio said that the Democratic Party is the biggest hate group in America. No words in current day American politics have ever spoken truer than that the Democratic Party is the biggest hate group. We need to expose the veneer in which these people have draped themselves for far too long, so that everyone can see them. These people constantly feel aggrieved, they never find happiness in anything. They never feel content. They are always on the lookout for the next victim group to "stand up" for. They never tire of constantly stirring up the masses with discontent.

Their arguments are old, tired, unimaginative, lazy and vindictive. They go something like the following. Republicans and conservatives want dirty air, they want sick people to die so that insurance companies can profit. Republicans want to take us back to the nineteen fifties, they want to take the vote away from black people. According to Nancy Pelosi they wish to starve babies.

When Democrats are not spreading demagoguery they are spitting vitriol. Why are these people always so enraged to where they will say the nastiest things, while pointing their fingers at everyone else? Maxine Waters has acted like a bonafide crazy woman in her response to the election of Donald Trump. She was calling for his impeachment before the man even took the oath of office. All of Trumps cabinet nominees were held up as some of the most insidious accusations flew out the mouths of Democrats against them.

These people are so filled with and blinded by hatred that they continue to dig themselves deeper, and deeper into a large pit filled with pig feces. During the confirmation hearings of Judge Gorsuch, they accused him of siding with corporations at the expense of the "little guy." There was no mention or interest in whether or not he upheld the constitution. Their only interest was in maintaining class warfare.

Trump's labor secretary was "an enemy of workers' rights," they predicted "a war on seniors" was coming with the confirmation of the Health and Human Services Secretary. Trump's Education Secretary nominee was about to "single-handedly decimate our public education system. Jeff Sessions was warned by Elizabeth Warren about "taking his "racism, sexism and bigotry" to the Justice Department. While Sessions was sitting with his grandchild who happened to be Asian American on his lap, while awaiting his confirmation as Attorney General, an MTV reporter told him to "take that toy back to toys are us."

One week after an insane hate filled Democrat supporter tried to take out Republican members of Congress, we had crazy Uncle Bernie telling a supporter to "fight back in an unprecedented way," assuring the supporter that because of the Health care bill that Republicans were currently working on "Thousands of people will die! He said, "There's no question in my mind. What kind of crazy world is it?"

Is it any wonder that you had this nut case heading out there shooting Republicans? After all if Republicans are responsible for the deaths of thousands, isn't violence justified against them?

What is wrong with these people? How long will they continue to get away with this type of behavior? They are always in a state of perpetual outrage. Democrats refuse to enforce immigration law and call those who wish to protect the borders racists. They are heavily invested in the race industry. They pit American's against each other; white against black, women against men, rich against poor. It never ends.

Who can forget the words of Hillary Clinton when she called millions of her countrymen a basket of deplorables, as she went on to quite casually, without any proof, label them as racist, sexist, homophobic, xenophobic, Islamophobic? She said that they are un-American and irredeemable, for no other reason than that they do not agree with her agenda. Hillary Clinton and the Democrats actually promoted the notion that with Donald Trump having the nuclear codes, it was actually conceivable that he would get us into a nuclear war because…wait for it…wait for it, because someone may get under his thin skin. Did you get that? Donald Trump would take us to nuclear war if somebody offends him! She said that, in all seriousness.

These people have to be rejected. On and on they go, decade after decade, year after year, month after month, week after week, day after day, hour aft… you get the point. This is a hate group that is not interested in ideas, only character assassination, vitriol and propaganda. Reject them! Look around, observe their behavior and categorically, utterly and unequivocally reject them until they change their methods.

The Democrat Party Clown Show

Wow, wow, wow! It was amazetacular!

The Democrat Party clown show was up and running during the last Presidential election, and boy, that gang was a riot. It was spectacular to behold! But unlike most regular clowns who desperately try to be funny and make you laugh, those clowns were serious, and they expected you to take them…joking aside.

As each Democrat clown entered onto the stage, a person was prepared to give every one of them a chance to make a case. After all, it was not supposed to be a clown show. The occasion was serious business. Without fail, as each one of them opened the mouth to speak, before you knew it, you found yourself rolling on the floor laughing.

It made no difference which one of them was on the stage, whether it was the communist millionaire complaining about "MMMMmillionaires and BBBBBillionaires," or the old privileged white guy apologizing for being an old privileged white guy. Those clowns had the audience unintentionally slapping their knees and grabbing their stomachs in uncontrollable laughter.

Just as one began to sober up from the drunkening effects of the side splitting laughter, along came the self-righteous religious gay zealot guy. He was telling everybody that they have to accept homosexuality as a legitimate lifestyle, otherwise God would strike them with a bolt of lightning. Kill 'em dead!

The fake Navajo then followed him, or was she Comanche Indian…or was it Cherokee, or…or…or Apache? Well whatever…the fake Native American, also worth millions of dollars, also railing against those "MMMillionaires and BBBBBillionaires"…in the most sanctimonious voice she could muster of course.

As that bunch made their way across the country, and eventually put away the pleasantries toward each other, they then got a little more serious. However, each time they attempted to do it, one had to ask, are these people really serious or are they pulling our legs again?

Who could forget the highfalutin former Deputy DA (she's now Vice President by the way) telling her drones that while she was in college, she once smoked weed to Tupac and Snoop Dog playing in the background? The thing is, when she was in college, neither Snoop nor Tupac had ever released any music. And by the time Snoop and Tupac had released their music she was already the Deputy DA. So she was either lying about smoking weed in college, or she simply mixed up the timeline, and she was smoking weed to Tupac and Snoop Dog while she was already a Deputy DA, probably putting people in jail for smoking weed.

One could be forgiven if at anytime one expected her to bust out with "you've been punked," but she never did. At that time you just had to accept that it was just a bad joke by the unfunny clown…maybe?

As they took their clown show all across the country the response was the same. Earlier on, they were all trying to see which one of them could be the most offended by a statement made by fellow presidential seat seeker and clown extraordinaire (now President) Joseph Biden.

Virtue was on full display as they each wagged their finger at old uncle Joe. No matter where they went, the response was the same from many in the country. People just had to shake their heads and laugh. Then the people were shaken with a sense of foreboding because they realized these clowns were serious. Those who recognized what was at stake did not know if to continue laughing or begin crying.

It did not matter! In the end, the clown extraordinaire beat all the other clowns. He became the champion clown for an office that required more gravitas.

No one is laughing now.

The Downright Nasty Democrat Party

Why is it that the most vicious, hateful, downright nasty people could so confidently walk around strutting, behaving like they are the examples of virtue? Any objective observer witnessing the behavior of the left and the Democrat Party over the last few years can see the unhinged, virulent, despicable and often violent way these people have behaved in pursuit of their agenda.

These people think that because they disagree politically with their opponents, that gives them the right to say anything about their opponents. They can make any accusations about others and people's character. They can behave in the most despicable manner that we have witnessed over the last few years. They have justified all of this because of their raw, unadulterated hatred of their political opponents. Yet these very people present themselves as the salt of the earth, and lights to the world.

How do you look at people like Nancy Pelosi, Chuck Schumer, Maxine Waters, and others who have been some of the nastiest people to ever hold political office and use them as examples of goodness and character?

You are morally outraged by Donald Trump, but Joe Biden is your example of integrity? How does one look at Alexander Ocasio Cortez, an absolutely mean spirited woman who is constantly demeaning people and accusing her political opponents of all kinds of wrongdoing, lying and casting aspersions on people's character in the attempt to destroy them politically, and then use her as an example of decency?

How does one look at people like "we are gonna impeach the MFer" Rashida Tlaib, and Elan Omar with admiration? These two women have shown their disdain for the people of Israel, but stay silent on atrocities committed by the Palestinians. They advocate for socialist policies and try to paint their opponents in the most unflattering colors?

How does one look at the Democrat Party and their culture of death, as they promote the cause of abortion up to the last day of pregnancy, and say yes; this is the party for me? How does one look at the constant attacks on people's freedom to worship, the attacks on free speech, the pernicious cancel culture, and the pushing of the warped transgender ideology even on little children, and say this is preferable?

This has to be a joke, but sadly, it is not. These people and their followers are so motivated and governed by hate that they have lost their capacity to discern right from wrong. We are all worse off for it. Good is now called evil, right is wrong, up is down, in is out, and back is front.

These people all walk around with no clothes on as their subjects lavish them with praise for their beautiful, fashionable outfits. This is madness.

MISCELLANEOUS

America is Becoming More Unrecognizable

The left and their media allies are truly dangerous. With their media allies doing their bidding, promulgating lies, spreading propaganda, and being silent in the face of absolute evil; this country is on a downward spiral. If we do not pull the brakes, we are going to end up in a really bad place.

It's sad to see. No one challenges the Press Secretary Psaki like they questioned the previous Press Secretary under the previous administration. No fact checks, and Joe Biden continues refusing to answer questions. Even as everyone continues to obsess over "violent white extremism," Antifa and BLM have been able to wreak havoc all over the country, and no one covers it except conservative media.

The low information crowd either dismisses all of it, or they do not even know what is happening. If people complain about injustice or chicanery by the government, but Google, YouTube, Facebook, Twitter and Instagram disagree, then their complaints will not be featured via any of the social media giants' platforms.

Never have we seen monopolies use their power so brazenly without fear of blowback. People can't even defend themselves on these platforms because the gods of social media decide what is true and what is not true. They decide who gets a voice.

Think about that for a moment. People can defame you, say anything against you before the world, but you cannot use the same mechanism to defend yourself. With the snap of a finger, the social media giants have the power to destroy anyone they deem a threat. You'll be deplatformed without warning or recourse.

It is crazy to observe what is going in America in 2021. This is part of what the Soviet Union did to their people for 70 years to suppress the masses. People love to use and trivialize the Nazi reference, but what we are witnessing now are real life Nazi tactics. The only difference is that now, instead of the Government; it is a few corporations who control the flow of information and decide what people should and should not hear.

They do all of this while being cheered on by a powerful political party that has decided freedom of speech in America is no longer a virtue and right worth protecting. They are not even ashamed.

Everything that these people accuse their political opponents of doing, they are guilty of being the chief proponents and actors of the charge they make.

We are living in an upside down world, back is front, outside is inside, black is white, white is black. Most alarming, evil is called goodness, and goodness is called evil.

The Fake 6 January 2021 "Insurrection"

We must say this really loud for everyone with ears to hear, for the sake of posterity. There was no insurrection attempt on 6 January 2021. A bunch of people went to the Capitol to protest what they believed to be a stole election was election. Whether there was election fraud is not the issue. The issue is that people believed there was fraud based on what they saw as irregularities during the elections in several states. They wanted to draw attention to it because none of the powers that be gave any attention to their concerns.

All citizens have the right to protest their government. Regardless of what anyone says, this is a pillar of the American Republic. It's not complicated and there is absolutely nothing wrong with it. People do not have to drop their concerns simply because others say they should. The protesters on 6 January had specific issues they were protesting...very specific claims they were making, and using their rights to draw attention to it.

In a very large crowd of tens of thousands of people, some thugs used intimidation and violence as a tactic. As many have said repeatedly, no right thinking person supports what happened that day, but there was no insurrection. It is a lie that the Democrat Party propagated in concert with the lying media to pursue impeachment, and militarize Washington D.C.

Think about how crazy the response has been. Washington D.C. became a militarized zone with tens of thousands of troops ready to fight against American citizens if someone determines it is necessary. Is there any scenario under which we would have imagined this a few short years ago? But hey, if there is the threat of an insurrection…

Do you understand how this works?

The difference in the response to the rioters on 6 January compared to the way people respond to violence on the left also says a lot. Violence is a tried-and-true tactic of the left and the Democrat Party underbelly. It never seems to matter though.

People condemn violence on the right. People excuse, cheer on, tolerate, and excuse violence on the left.

The attitude on the left is that their violence is righteous, violence for a worthy cause. If you have a different opinion, be careful, they will also commit acts of violence against you.

What happened on 6 January 2021 was a rare incident. It was a horrible incident that will leave a dark stain in the nation's history. It was however an incident, as opposed to a way of life that is practiced like we see all the time on the left.

Don't get it confused. From the arrests that have happened so far, among the rioters there was also a significant Antifa presence. It is part of their modus operandi to infiltrate protests and stir up trouble. You will never know this though, because the corrupt media features none of this news.

Is it any wonder, that "news organizations" like CNN actively campaign to block out news organizations like OAN, Epoch Times, Newsmax and even Fox News (even though Fox has started to swing left)?

These are crazy times indeed.

The FBI investigation into the Obama Presidency

The year is 2008. Barack Obama has just won the Presidency. Before he could even take the oath of office, there is talk that he is not a natural born American citizen of the U.S. The emphasis is that as a result, his election to the highest office in the land is null and void. Officials, reporters and other operatives immediately go into action to lend validity to the claim that Obama is not a U.S. citizen. They make these claims based on nothing. There is no evidence whatsoever that Obama is not an American citizen. However, the media, Hollywood, officials in the Government, and pundits everywhere continue to push the conspiracy that Obama is not an American citizen.

Obama protests! He cannot understand why everyone is making such a claim, and so many people are giving it credence. He calls it a witch hunt.

Obama lashes out at those spreading the completely false notion, and the promulgation that he is not a U.S. citizen. Obama accuses his opponents of using baseless accusations and tactics to try to remove him from power. He even blurts out again and again that the effort to delegitimize his election win is a witch hunt, and a major hoax.

Despite Obama's protestations though, the fabrication persists and his opponents seem to go into a feeding frenzy at the prospect of destroying his Presidency before it even gets underway. His opponents smell blood! They move in like sharks to politically destroy him completely. Before you know it, the justice department launches an investigation to determine if President Obama is indeed a legitimate American citizen, and eligible to hold the highest office in the land.

The investigation is launched strictly on innuendo that he was born in Kenya, nothing else…just innuendo. No one ever presented any evidence whatsoever to justify the investigation. It was just launched based on nothing but a hunch that it is true. Would you believe it? They appointed a trusted swamp creature to head up the investigation. The person truly in the lead however, is an old Democrat Party nemesis. He truly despises the Democrat Party and has worked for the Republican Party as one of their biggest advocates. Working alongside him are 13 fierce Republican loyalists.

The media then loops the story 24/7, and the narrative is that Obama must be a Kenyan citizen. Guest after guest on the nightly news shows predicts assuredly that Obama''s Presidency is doomed because he is illegitimate.

As the conspiracy gains legs, then wheels, then wings, it never produces one shred of evidence is ever produced that Obama was born in Kenya. Every time they breathlessly proclaimed that this time they've got the goods, it proves to be fake news…over and over again. Nevertheless,

Congressmen, Senators, the former CIA director, the former FBI director, the former NSA director and others in authority lead the charge that Barrack Obama is not the legitimate President of the United States.

He is beholden to the country of Kenya.

The issue is no longer being treated as speculation, but as certainty. Before you know it, Congress is threatening to impeach him for his deceit.

Everyone insists that it must be true that Obama is not a citizen. They come to this conclusion because in the past, Obama had referenced his desire to learn more about Kenya. It is because his father was from and he still has relatives in that country. Obama even tried to buy a house in Kenya at one time.

The country then finds out that shortly after Obama announced he was running for President in 2007, the Bush Administration placed an FBI mole in Obama's campaign to find evidence that he indeed was not born in America. As time went by, more information came out that the Bush administration used the FBI mole to plant information saying the Kenyans have proof Obama was indeed born in Kenya.

One low level Obama staffer casually mentions to another person in conversation what the FBI mole said about the Kenyans having proof that Obama was born in Kenya. The FBI then uses the information that they planted, that the Obama staffer then repeated, as a reason to launch further investigations into Obama's campaign. But that is not all. John McCain who is running against Obama, hires a company to do opposition research on the Obama campaign, using a former British spy who openly expressed disdain for Obama, and his desire to see Obama lose the election.

The company that hires the British spy, using Kenyan disinformation specialists, produces a dossier filled with spectacular and salacious accusations about Obama. The former British spy clarifies he cannot verify anything in the dossier. But the dossier produced by the company hired by the McCain campaign, is then used by the FBI to look deeper into Obama's campaign anyway.

One high level FBI official makes it clear the dossier is unreliable. It is opposition research paid for by the McCain campaign, but other officials higher up in the FBI use the dossier anyway to get a warrant from the Federal Investigation Surveillance Act (FISA) courts to further investigate Obama's campaign.

The FBI officials deceive the courts by claiming that the information is verified and reliable, which leads to the government surveillance of Obama's campaign, long before the justice Department's investigation even starts.

Throughout the journey, Obama persisted in his protest, demonstrating the dignified manner for which he is renowned. He continued to claim racism, and call it a hoax and a witch hunt, but his deprecators bizarrely claim that by protesting so vociferously, he was obstructing justice.

The story gets even more convoluted, but there is not enough room for all the details in this short retelling of the story. Just know that for the next two and a half years the country got caught up in the intrigue of Obama's birth certificate. As a result many citizens gave short shrift to all the terrific things happening in the economy, other domestic issues, and foreign affairs.

Poor Barrack, imagine using the levers of government power to go after him like that. Who would have thought this could happen in the United States of America?

Deflecting

Imagine you are an EMT. You get summoned to the scene of a horrific accident. You get rid of the Starbucks coffee you've been sipping on for the last hour. It's been a slow morning, but suddenly there's some excitement. This is why you are an EMT. You know the dangers of the world we live in and you want to do your part to help make it a better place for everyone.

As you pull out, sirens piercing, adrenaline pumping, and you get more information about the accident, you push down on the accelerator even harder. You get to the scene of the accident and you immediately get a sense of how terrible the situation is. It's worse than you thought! The seriousness of it shakes you to the core. No matter, you do not freeze up. You are a professional. Like the pro that you are, you begin to assess the situation to determine where you are needed most.

There are dead bodies lying all around. Some people have suffered severe injuries. Some are bleeding profusely, some are unconscious, others have broken bones, some are in shock. The scene of the tragedy is really dreadful, but in the midst of all the horror, you also notice that some of the people involved in the accident escaped with some injuries that are not as bad as the others. They definitely need medical help. Meanwhile, they can apply some self care. Do what they can to ease their situation and perhaps bear the discomfort until more help arrives.

As you and your team apply first aid to those who need it the most, one of the people who is not so badly injured begins to complain that you are not treating the scratches on his face. Another man walks over to you while you are treating an injured child bleeding profusely on the ground. The man complains that he has a really substantial bump on his forehead, and he needs you to turn your attention to him. He is distracting you as you try to stop the bleeding on the child. You ask the man with the bump on his forehead to step back. He walks over to another member of your team and complains to the technician applying life saving CPR on another victim of the accident.

As mentioned earlier, these other people also need medical attention, but it is your team's responsibility to concentrate on the other priority patients. Losing patience, as you continue to treat the patients who really need your lifesaving skills, the less injured people complain you are ignoring their injuries. They continue to hinder you from doing your job.

You try appealing to their sense of reason by pointing to all the people who badly need your attention more than they do. However, it makes no difference to the people harassing you as you try to do your job. They will not listen and they accuse you of deflecting. They claim that for other reasons, you really do not want to help them. You are just using all of those badly injured people as excuses to avoid helping them.

Of course, this is not a real scenario, and it is hard to imagine anything like this ever really happening, but this can be likened to some segments of black America, but with a slight twist.

Many black Americans keep complaining about the lesser injuries, and sometimes deaths that occasionally come at the hands of the police. They ignore all of the bleeding and mayhem taking place in their own communities.

They look at the thousands of dead bodies, the carnage, the chaos and the mayhem caused by other black people taking place in their own streets, and they don't seem to be bothered by those issues as much. The only thing that matters to these black people is when something unfortunate happens with the police, or some act of racism.

When sober-minded people try to point out that anger over police misconduct is understood, but it is not as big a problem as black people think it is, too many black people become even angrier. When people point out that addressing the problem of black on black violence is an issue that is exponentially larger, and that needs more urgent attention than police brutality; too many black people accuse those pointing this out of deflecting. And the vicious cycle continues.

Facts do not matter to them. What matters more than anything is basking in, and maintaining the posture of the victim.

Oh well, that's just deflecting.

The Duplicity of a Banana Peel

In August 2017 at the University of Mississippi, an atrocity of epic proportions transpired. The incident left people traumatized beyond measure. Four years later, and many still carry the scars from the incident. They are unsure if they can, or ever will recover from the tragedy of that day at their esteemed university.

Many young leaders from the Ole Miss Greek life were at the school to attend a retreat "designed to build leaders and bring the campus closer together." Everything was on track for a magnificent weekend of mentoring, learning, and character building. Suddenly, without warning, an act so cold disrupted the event and brought it to an abrupt end. All the effort that was put into planning and making the event a memorable success would be for naught, as it had to be cancelled.

Students and campus authorities had to deal with an act of pure hatred so vile that people are still in shock all these years later. This was such a repulsive deed that students had to retreat to their safe spaces in order to deal adequately with the trauma caused by the act. So, what happened that was so terrible it brought a planned retreat to come to an end before it ever began? Brace yourselves everyone! This is blood-curdling stuff. Now is the time to stop reading if you have a weak stomach.

You've been warned!

The three-day event was cut short on the evening of the first day. They cut it short after three black students found a banana peel in a tree in front of a cabin at the camp. You read that right folks, but just in case you are wondering if you did read it right, be assured that you did. Nevertheless, to save you the trouble of looking back, let's repeat it.

Three black students spotted a banana peel in a tree in front of one cabin at the camp. Because of the sighting, the event that was planned for those three days was brought to an abrupt end.

For an entire day, the student's discovery ignited a vigorous discussion about "symbolism," and reports indicate that the discussion sometimes became heated. During the discussion, one student revealed that because he could not find an available trashcan in proximity, he simply threw the peel in the tree. Even after finding out how the peel got in the tree, reports state that some students left the retreat in tears. One Greek leader claimed that because of the incident, students did not feel welcome or safe. Many others "were hurt, frightened and upset" by the incident. She spoke of the paranoia that she felt after seeing the banana peel.

This is part of what one of the school's staff said in a letter addressing student leadership, according to the school's student newspaper: "Because of the underlying reality many students of color endure on a daily basis, the conversation manifested into a larger conversation about race relations today at the University of Mississippi." The guilty student offered a heartfelt apology for the unintentionally callous manner in which he disposed of the banana peel, and he stressed that there was no excuse for the pain that he caused, though his action was not in any way an attack against any one or group. "I have much to learn and look forward to doing such and encourage all members of our community to do the same," he said.

This incident ladies and gentlemen clearly illustrates why so many people of color adaadoptpt the victim mentality in this country. University campuses all across the country harness and cultivate this mentality, making young people feel that there is virtue in being a victim and being weak. Being frightened by a banana peel is pathetic. Developing paranoia, feeling hurt and upset because of a banana peel in a tree is ludicrous.

Think about this for one moment folks. What mindset must people possess to jump automatically to the conclusion that a banana peel in a tree is some kind of attack on black people? How does an individual's mind become so enchained, that this kind of response to such an innocuous incident is considered reasonable? This is another prime example of the soft bigotry of low expectations. The people who cast themselves as protectors believe black people are so weak, they cannot handle a banana peel carelessly flung into the branches of a tree.

Those who encourage this ridiculous attitude see themselves as enlightened, as being conscious of the struggle, they are "woke." Truth is these people are a major part of the problem because, instead of telling young people to grow up, stop whining and feeling sorry for themselves, they encourage them to feel sorry for themselves and throw pity parties. They do black people and other minorities no favors by encouraging them to wallow in the mud of victimhood. Far worse than helping, they do the country no favors by encouraging this behavior. Because of this attitude that is promoted by professors, staff and other leadership at these college campuses, so many people who live blessed lives end up leaving these institutions with a chip on their shoulder. They carry them around because professors, staff, and other leadership at these college campuses teach them, despite their everyday experience, that they are victims who are at a natural disadvantage for no other reason than the color of their skin.

It is no wonder that in two thousand and seventeen and beyond, when there are so many laws in place to fight discrimination, when people and businesses can be sued for millions of dollars, when government agencies like the Equal Employment Opportunity Commission exists to combat discrimination, when businesses all across the country have dedicated Human Resources Departments to fight discrimination, and when the worst thing one could be called is a racist, people still believe that "the system" is out to get them.

Too many white people who have no reason to feel guilty for misdeeds that black people, or "people of color" have suffered in the past, get caught up in these silly ventures into political correctness. They constantly try to assuage the guilt imposed on them. They try to compensate for it by treating black people and others as their special projects. In order to feel good about themselves, they infantilize black people and others. They appoint themselves as their protectors, and in the process do nothing but keep the people who they think they are helping from rising to the heights that they can really ascend. After all, these people whom they wish to help are victims, right?

It is time for many black people to snap out of the state of mind that a victim posture, and a weak disposition are positions of virtue. You are no different than any other American. You too are God's creation, with tons of latent ability just yearning to rise to the surface so that you too can excel. It is time to stop falling for the ploys that seek to make you continue to embrace the victim mentality.

Break free of those chains and live your life as God intended. It is high time.

A Trip Down Memory Lane With Memories Of A Rodeo Clown

Does anyone remember the rodeo clown who dressed up like President Obama back in 2011 at the Wisconsin State Fair? In the past, the clown had dressed up like other Presidents, and made fun of them just the same. This case was different though.

This one went down as one of the all time classics in white guilt/black victimhood. It served as one of the quintessential examples of media hypocrisy during the time of President Trump. People should never forget this one.

The clown who had no idea that the America of President Barrack Obama did not allow such sacrilege, was about to find out what it was like to blaspheme the holy one of America. He was to learn that his act of blasphemy was punishable by the powerful guardians of his holiness Barrack.

How dare this, this…this…this rodeo clown think that he could make fun of…sound the trumpet…the first black President of the United States (feel the tingle run down your spine as one says those precious words). Such acts were forbidden, but this rodeo clown never got the memo. Though the sacred proclamation had gone out several times before in the media and elsewhere, he never got the memo.

One Obama disciple exclaimed that it was "like some kind of Klan rally you'd see on TV." Another disciple said "It wasn't clean; it wasn't fun. It was awful; it was sickening. It was racist."

The response to the clown's transgression was swift, the punishment severe. It did not matter that people had made similar depictions of past Presidents before. That was free speech doggone it! When a rodeo clown decides to perform the same act, in the same lighthearted manner as it had been done in the past, but this time with the black guy occupying the white house; there are no excuses. He ought to have known better. It is self-evident as the sun rising in the East. You do not make fun of the black President.

The media had a field day following the incident. CNN doing what they do best (bringing us the news that matter), treated the story like the aftermath of the 11 September 2001 attacks against the twin towers in New York City. For the next week they pushed the story, lamenting, complaining, and questioning what a horrible, evil, racist country the United States is.

They had guests aplenty who gave credence to the idea that this otherwise unknown rodeo clown who had performed the same act before was a scourge to society, and that he needed to be forever banished from the shores of the United States to an uninhabited unknown planet outside our galaxy. For his sins, this previously unknown rodeo clown, who (just in case you missed it) had done the same act before with other sitting Presidents, was banned for life from participating in the Missouri State fair.

He begged for forgiveness, but there would be no redemption. This was the political equivalent of the unforgivable sin. They would not, could not grant him redemption! The president of the Missouri Rodeo Cowboy Association resigned, and according to reports, had his life threatened for being the enabler of the transgressor clown.

Those who disapproved of the clown's actions bombarded him from every direction. The man was in such a state of panic that he thought he would lose his job as Superintendent of the school district where he worked. His lawyer said "He's shaking like a small dog passing razor blades."

According to CNN, the Missouri State Fair Commission said that before it will consider contracting with the association again, "They must provide evidence to the director of the Missouri State Fair that they have proof that all officials and subcontractors of the MRCA have successfully participated in sensitivity training." Yes folks, you read that right, sensitivity training, or as they called it in the former Soviet Union when people dared to challenge the authority, re-education camp.

This is what happened a long time ago in America's history…oh no wait a minute, this is just a few years ago during the reign of Barrack The First, also known as Barack The Great, also referred to as THE MOHSSST DISS-REE-SPECKTED PRESIDENT EVAH! He was even more disrespected than George W. Bush. By the way, for anyone interested, Bush was famously known as the dumb President, but let us not digress any further.

Fast forward just a few months after the reign of the great one. When a rapper said to the sitting President: "you'd better shut your mouth before I pimp your wife" the reaction is crickets. When a State lawmaker says that the President is guaranteed to not serve out his full term, especially if the lawmaker gets near him, the response is, meh no big deal! When 67 congressmen boycotted the inauguration of the President, he brought it on himself.

When popular celebrities talk about thoughts of blowing up the white house, who cares, these people don't matter. When celebrities threaten to beat the sitting President with a baseball bat, and a couple more portray themselves doing violence to the President in their music videos and plays, and another one talks about suffocating him with a pillow, that is all free speech. These attacks continued for four years.

Well, we understand. This is all acceptable behavior because the guy in the white house was not a Democrat, right? Besides, it served him right. This automatically makes the behavior acceptable. Second, he is not black, and most significant of all he is an old white male. He is from that one demographic that Americans can say anything about, no matter how despicable.

He deserved the treatment that he got, after all; in the eyes of his detractors, that guy was just a rodeo clown anyway.

ABOUT THE AUTHOR

The author is originally from Trinidad and Tobago, the most southerly of the Caribbean, West Indian archipelago, nine miles off the coast of Venezuela from the closest point. Like so many immigrants who have come to the United States, he understands how blessed he is to live here.

He migrated over 25 years ago and says that his life was never the same from the first day that he set his feet on American soil. He says he was blown away by the sheer grandeur of the place, and utterly amazed that so much opportunities to be successful existed for anyone who was willing to put in the work.

For a poor, uneducated immigrant who prior to arriving in America, was never able to make much progress in his life, America was everything that he thought it would be.

He has a Master of Science in Administration degree, a Bachelor's degree in Organizational Management, has worked for the U.S. Government and has written some articles for a prominent government organization.

The hatred that so many Americans have for their own country has always taken aback the author. The explosion of noxious anti-American sentiments by American citizens continue to baffle him.

The constant appeal to race and the incessant effort to paint the country as a downright evil nation that has contributed nothing to the world, and has made no progress since the days of slavery, often leaves him scratching his head. He quite frequently finds himself wondering if the minds of the complainers exist in an alternate universe while their bodies are simply refined zombie manifestations walking around the country.

He sometimes believes that one of these days, even after all of these years, he'll awaken to half of the country standing over his bed. Everyone will be grabbing their stomachs, slapping their knees and thighs, flinging their heads back, laughing uncontrollably, pointing their fingers and screaming "you've been punked."

REFERENCES

admin. (2017, May 18). Trump Impeachment Talk Started Before He Was Even Nominated. True Pundit. https://truepundit.com/trump-impeachment-talk-started-before-he-was-even-nominated/

Archive, V. A., feed, G. author R., Archive, V. A., & feed, G. author R. (2021, October 29). Lincoln Project claims responsibility for fake "white supremacists" at Glenn Youngkin event. New York Post. https://nypost.com/2021/10/29/glenn-youngkin-aide-accuses-terry-mcauliffe-team-of-fake-white-supremacist-stunt/

Bates, T. (n.d.). Misusing "Separation of Church and State." The Heritage Foundation. Retrieved December 8, 2021, from https://www.heritage.org/civilrights/commentary/misusing-separation-church-and-state

Bauman, V. (2010, April 12). Foes of tea party movement to infiltrate rallies. The Seattle Times. https://www.seattletimes.com/seattle-news/politics/foes-of-tea-party-movement-to-infiltrate-rallies/

Boyle, M. (2016, June 21). Orlando Terrorist Supported Hillary Clinton to Stop Donald Trump. Breitbart. https://www.breitbart.com/politics/2016/06/21/orlando-terrorist-supported-hillary-clinton-to-stop-donald-trump/

Bykofsky, S. (n.d.). Can whites be trusted? Black law prof says no | Stu Bykofsky. Https://Www.inquirer.com. Retrieved December 8, 2021, from https://www.inquirer.com/philly/columnists/stu_bykofsky/can-white-be-trusted-black-law-prof-says-no-stu-bykofsky-20171114.html

CBS News. (2015, August 31). "Pigs in a blanket" chant at Minnesota Fair riles police. Cbsnews.com. https://www.cbsnews.com/news/pigs-in-a-blanket-chant-at-minnesota-fair-riles-police/

Chamberlain, S. (2021, June 4). NYC shrink tells Yale audience she fantasizes about shooting white people in head. New York Post. https://nypost.com/2021/06/04/nyc-pyscho-fantasizes-about-shooting-white-people-in-yale-talk/

CNN, J. L. (n.d.). After Obama-mocking rodeo clown, Missouri fair requires "sensitivity training." CNN. Retrieved December 14, 2021, from http://edition.cnn.com/2013/08/15/politics/missouri-rodeo-clowns-sensitivity-training-obama-clown/index.html

Column: Larry Elder is the Black face of white supremacy. You've been warned. (2021, August 20). Los Angeles Times. https://www.latimes.com/california/story/2021-08-20/recall-candidate-larry-elder-is-a-threat-to-black-californians

Conklin, A. (2021, April 28). BLM co-founder repeatedly praised convicted cop-killer Assata Shakur. Fox News. https://www.foxnews.com/us/blm-co-founder-praised-asata-shakur

Conservative Stacey Dash FIRES BACK After Chelsea Handler Calls Her A "Black White Supremacist." (n.d.). The Daily Wire. Retrieved December 8, 2021, from https://www.dailywire.com/news/conservative-stacey-dash-fires-back-after-chelsea-amanda-prestigiacomo

"Death To America" tweets Kansas University student body president. (n.d.). Www.americanthinker.com. Retrieved December 8, 2021, from https://www.americanthinker.com/blog/2021/09/death_to_a merica_tweets_kansas_university_student_body_president. html

Democrats own the violence and riots in their cities. (2020, August 31). Washington Examiner. https://www.washingtonexaminer.com/opinion/democrats-own-the-violence-and-riots-in-their-cities

Dinesh D'Souza. (2016, July 13). Dinesh D'Souza: The secret history of the Democratic Party. Fox News; Fox News. https://www.foxnews.com/opinion/dinesh-dsouza-the-secret-history-of-the-democratic-party

Dorfman, Z. (n.d.). Why Did Obama Free This Terrorist? POLITICO Magazine. Retrieved December 8, 2021, from https://www.politico.com/magazine/story/2017/01/oscar-lopez-commutation-barack-obama-214685/

Douglas MacArthur. (2014, April 3). Biography. https://www.biography.com/political-figure/douglas-macarthur

Drexel University professor under fire for "white genocide" tweet. (n.d.). Www.cbsnews.com. Retrieved December 8, 2021, from

https://www.cbsnews.com/news/drexel-university-professor-under-fire-for-white-genocide-tweet/

Fresno shooting rampage: Suspected gunman wanted to kill as many white people as possible, cops say. (2017, April 19). Fox News. https://www.foxnews.com/us/fresno-shooting-rampage-suspected-gunman-wanted-to-kill-as-many-white-people-as-possible-cops-say

Golden, C. D. (2019, October 26). Never Forget a Rodeo Clown Was Fired Over an Obama Mask but Pics of Trump Being Killed Are Apparently Fine. The Western Journal.

https://www.westernjournal.com/never-forget-rodeo-clown-fired-obama-mask-pics-trump-killed-apparently-fine/

Good, C. (2010, August 10). A Hilariously Inept Attempt at Actual Tea Party Infiltration. The Atlantic.

https://www.thcatlantic.com/politics/archive/2010/08/a-hilariously-inept-attempt-at-actual-tea-party-infiltration/61226/

Gravity - Stephen Hawking says universe can create itself from nothing, but how exactly? (n.d.). Physics Stack Exchange. Retrieved December 8, 2021, from

https://physics.stackexchange.com/questions/13013/stephen-hawking-says-universe-can-create-itself-from-nothing-but-how-exactly

Hanchett, I. (2017, December 29). WaPo's Tumulty: "Every Fifth Grader Could Tell You That Climate Change Refers to Unpredictable Weather Patterns." Breitbart. https://www.breitbart.com/clips/2017/12/29/wapos-tumulty-every-fifth-grader-could-tell-you-that-climate-change-refers-to-unpredictable-weather-patterns/

History.com Editors. (2018, August 21). Paris Peace Accords signed. HISTORY. https://www.history.com/this-day-in-history/paris-peace-accords-signed

HistoryNet Staff. (2001, October 2). President William McKinley: Assassinated by an Anarchist. HistoryNet; HistoryNet. https://www.historynet.com/president-william-mckinley-assassinated-by-an-anarchist.htm

How Blacks became Democratic: The Myth of Republican Racism. (2013, March 26). Soul Therapy. https://dathistoryguy.wordpress.com/2013/03/26/how-blacks-became-democratic-the-myth-of-republican-racism/

https://twitter.com/foxnews/status/931346346308759552. (n.d.). Twitter. Retrieved December 8, 2021, from https://twitter.com/FoxNews/status/931346346308759552

https://www.washingtontimes.com, T. W. T. (n.d.). Saida Grundy, Boston University professor: White males a "problem population." The Washington Times. Retrieved December 8, 2021, from

https://www.washingtontimes.com/news/2015/may/9/saida-grundy-boston-university-professor-white-mal/

Huston, W. T. (2017, June 30). Acts of Terror: A History of Left-Wing Political Violence in America. Breitbart. https://www.breitbart.com/politics/2017/06/30/acts-of-terror-history-of-left-wing-political-violence-in-america/

Jake Tapper admits Trump didn't call coronavirus a "hoax" after failing to correct AOC's claim. (2020, March 22). Washington Examiner. https:/www.washingtonexaminer.com/news/jake-tapper-admits-trump-didnt-call-coronavirus-a-hoax-after-failing-to-correct-aocs-claim

Joe Biden Brags about getting Ukranian Prosecutor Fired. (n.d.). Www.youtube.com. Retrieved December 8, 2021, from https://www.youtube.com/watch?v=UXA--dj2-CY

Joyce, F. (2015, December 22). White men must be stopped: The very future of mankind depends on it. Salon. https://www.salon.com/2015/12/22/white_men_must_be_stopped_the_very_future_of_the_planet_depends_on_it_partner/

Kaplan, T. (2020, September 1). Walker claims Biden, Democrats "trying to flip the script" on urban riots: "They know they're in trouble." Fox News. https://www.foxnews.com/politics/scott-walker-biden-democrats-flip-script-riots

Keller, M. (2018, September 10). Maxine Waters mocks: I threaten Trump supporters "all the time." TheHill. https://thehill.com/homenews/house/405877-maxine-waters-i-threaten-trump-supporters-all-the-time kemberlee-kaye. (2018, August 16). Hillary Clinton Praises 11-Year-Old Who Kneeled During Pledge of Allegiance. Le·gal In·sur·rec·tion |; Le·gal In·sur·rec·tion. https://legalinsurrection.com/2018/08/hillary-clinton-praises-11-year-old-who-kneeled-during-pledge-of-allegiance/

Lena Dunham's Sick-Making Skit Celebrates Extinction of Straight White Males. (n.d.). The Daily Wire. Retrieved December 8, 2021, from

https://www.dailywire.com/news/lena-dunhams-sick-making-skit-celebrates-amanda-prestigiacomo

Maxine Waters: The Lover of Marxism Who Hates President Trump - Frontpagemag. (n.d.). Www.frontpagemag.com. Retrieved December 8, 2021, from

https://www.frontpagemag.com/fpm/2020/04/maxine-waters-lover-marxism-who-hates-president-discover-networks/

Nast, C. (2019, October 11). Maxine Waters Has Called for Impeachment Since 2017. Fellow Democrats, Welcome to the Party. Glamour.

https://www.glamour.com/story/maxine-waters-impeachment-interview

News, A. B. C. (n.d.). At Least 217 Arrested, Limo Torched Amid Trump Inauguration Day Protests in Washington. ABC News. Retrieved December 8, 2021, from https://abcnews.go.com/Politics/arrests-violence-flares-parts-capital-inauguration-day/story?id=44925970

Nolte, J. (2011, November 16). Could a Possible #OccupyWallStreet Connection Explain Lack of MSM's White House Shooting Coverage? Breitbart. https://www.breitbart.com/the-media/2011/11/16/could-a-possible-occupywallstreet-connection-explain-lack-of-msms-white-house-shooting-coverage/

"Not Our President": Protests Spread After Donald Trump's Election. (2016, November 10). The New York Times. https://www.nytimes.com/2016/11/10/us/trump-election-protests.html

Oscar Lopez Rivera: Hero Or Terrorist? (n.d.). Www.youtube.com. Retrieved December 8, 2021, from https://www.youtube.com/watch?v=cAdJ-WPeHA4

President Ronald Reagan: A Soldier's Pledge. (n.d.). Www.youtube.com. Retrieved December 8, 2021, from https://www.youtube.com/watch?v=oqRGQ2jSsoc

Protesters Chant "What Do We Want, Dead Cops." (n.d.). Www.youtube.com. Retrieved December 8, 2021, from https://www.youtube.com/watch?v=h-dr_IhQu-I

reagan.com. (n.d.). Www.reagan.com. https://www.reagan.com/ronald-reagan-freedom-speech

Rolling Stone Busted and Shamed For Writing Fakest "Horse Dewormer" Story You'll Ever See. (n.d.). Retrieved December 8, 2021, from https://waynedupree.com/2021/09/rolling-stone-fake-news-story/?yptr=yahoo

Round Up The Rodeo Clowns: NAACP Official Calls For Rodeo Employees To Be Prosecuted For Hate Crime. (2013, August 16). JONATHAN TURLEY. https://jonathanturley.org/2013/08/16/round-up-the-rodeo-clowns-naacp-official-calls-for-rodeo-employees-to-be-prosecuted-for-hate-crime/comment-page-5/ Schoen, J. W. (2017, February 24). Donald Trump sets record for delay in getting Cabinet approved. Www.cnbc.com. https://www.cnbc.com/2017/02/24/trumps-cabinet-waiting-for-confirmation.html

Shadwick, L. (2015, August 28). Black Activists Call for Lynching and Hanging of White People and Cops. Breitbart. https://www.breitbart.com/border/2015/08/28/black-activists-called-for-lynching-and-hanging-of-white-people-and-cops/

Snowfall: "A very rare and exciting event." (n.d.). Dailycaller.com. Retrieved December 8, 2021, from https://dailycaller.com/2010/12/24/snowfall-a-very-rare-and-exciting-event/

Sordid History of Dem Party Against Blacks (Must Read) – John McTernan's Insights. (n.d.). Defendproclaimthefaith.org. Retrieved December 8, 2021, from https://defendproclaimthefaith.org/blog/sordid-history-of-dem-party-against-blacks-must-read/

Staff, G. (2018, June 14). The unspeakable truth about slavery in Mauritania. The Guardian; The Guardian. https://www.theguardian.com/global-development/2018/jun/08/the-unspeakable-truth-about-slavery-in-mauritania

Stranahan, L. (2015, September 10). F*** Yo Flag Movement Calls For Black Lives Matter Violence On 9/11. Breitbart. https://www.breitbart.com/politics/2015/09/09/fukyoflag-movement-calls-for-black-lives-matter-violence-on-911/

The Root Institute 2021: Understanding CRT. (n.d.). The Root. Retrieved December 8, 2021, from

https://www.theroot.com/the-root-institute-2021-unpacking-the-attacks-on-criti-1847711634

"They're Not Welcome Anymore, Anywhere." Maxine Waters Tells Supporters to Confront Trump Officials. (n.d.). Www.yahoo.com. https://news.yahoo.com/apos-apos-not-welcome-anymore-114523010.html?fr=yhssrp_catchall

Thornton, C. 'BIG C. (2021, March 24). Kamala Harris' Niece Under Fire Stating: "Violent White Men Are the Greatest Terrorist Threat to Our Country," Where's the Lie? Black Enterprise. https://www.blackenterprise.com/kamala-harris-niece-under-fire-stating-violent-white-men-are-the-greatest-terrorist-threat-to-our-country-wheres-the-lie/

Times, D. A. S. S. T. the N. Y. (1967, March 28). Saudi Arabian Slavery Persists Despite Ban by Faisal in 1962. The New York Times.
https://www.nytimes.com/1967/03/28/archives/saudi-arabian-slavery-persists-despite-ban-by-faisal-in-1962.html

Trump Didn't Call Neo-Nazis "Fine People." Here's Proof. | RealClearPolitics. (2019). Realclearpolitics.com.

https://www.realclearpolitics.com/articles/2019/03/21/trump_didnt_call_neo-nazis_fine_people_heres_proof_139815.html

Trump's wait for his major Cabinet picks was nearly the longest in 30 years. (n.d.). Washington Post. https://www.washingtonpost.com/graphics/politics/how-long-confirmations-will-take/

Video of BLM protesters chanting popular Iranian phrase "Death to America" goes viral. (2020, September 1). Washington Examiner. https://www.washingtonexaminer.com/news/video-of-blm-protesters-chanting-popular-iranian-phrase-death-to-america-goes-viral

(n.d.). Video Shows NYC Protesters Chanting for "Dead Cops." NBC New York. Retrieved December 8, 2021, from https://www.nbcnewyork.com/news/local/eric-garner-manhattan-dead-cops-video-millions-march-protest/2015303/

Why Do Liberals Defend Black Cop-Killers Like Mumia Abu-Jamal and Assata Shakur? (2021, June 7). Www.theepochtimes.com. https://www.theepochtimes.com/why-do-liberals-defend-black-cop-killers-like-mumia-abu-jamal-and-assante-shakur_3848590.html

You'll Never Guess Which Presidential Candidate Muslim Terrorist Omar Mateen Supported. (n.d.). Dailycaller.com. Retrieved December 8, 2021, from https://dailycaller.com/2016/06/21/omar-mateen-liked-hillary-clinton-informant-says/

I'd love to know what your reading experience with this book has been. I'd be grateful to hear from you, and for you to tell me what you think.

Please Leave a review. If you would like to say more, send a message to the email below Email: upoppolitics@gmail.com

I'd love to know what your reading experience with this book has been. I'd be grateful to hear from you, and for you to tell me what you think. I encourage your feedback.

Please leave a review. If you would like to say more, feel free to engage with me at the email below: Email:

upoppolitics@gmail.com